STICKS & STONES | STEEL & GLASS

UNBRIDLED BOOKS

Anthony Poon

ONE ARCHITECT'S JOURNEY

STICKS & STONES | STEEL & GLASS

UNBRIDLED BOOKS

Library of Congress Cataloging-in-Publication Data

Names: Poon, Anthony, 1964- author.
Title: Sticks & stones/steel & glass / by Anthony Poon.
Other titles: Sticks and stones, steel and glass
Description: Lakewood, CO : Unbridled Books, 2017.
Identifiers: LCCN 2016033491 | ISBN 9781609531362 (paperback)
Subjects: LCSH: Poon, Anthony, 1964—Themes, motives. | BISAC:
ARCHITECTURE
/ Individual Architects & Firms / General.
Classification: LCC NA737.P57 A35 2017 | DDC 720—dc23
LC record available at https://lccn.loc.gov/2016033491

1 3 5 7 9 10 8 6 4 2

Book Design by SH • CV

First Printing

CONTENTS

AUTHOR'S NOTE

I'VE DESIGNED a massive library and a sports complex, sprawling homes and stylish restaurants, projects that took years—and yet this book has been my most difficult project. Not that I have secrets to tell, and I hope nothing here sounds like I'm full of myself. I try openly to laugh at my mistakes. But I do want to see the larger meanings in my life's work.

The thing is, a book like this is not a straight line from my T-square. Whatever blueprint I started with has changed dozens of times midconstruction. Critiques I wrote a few years ago lost their steam over time and were dropped, while new projects shed a fresh light on topics I wanted to address in words as well as in lines and angles.

There was a time early on when this book was just a diary in which I wanted to write outrageously about architecture, as Anthony Bourdain did about cooking in *Kitchen Confidential*. Silly me. This book is not a memoir but rather is (somewhat) the trace of my life, my journey in the world of architecture and design—though it is not chronological.

I revel in the scope of exploration; I want to design everything, to be deeply invested in all creative aspects of a project. I want each minute or broad stroke of my architecture and design work to facilitate enriched lives for all who walk through the doors or look in or out of the windows of anything I create. And I celebrate that I have been allowed to sketch out visions for uplifting structures. Once I did so alongside a spiritual leader totally at peace with himself.

Something I'm still striving to be.

STICKS & STONES | STEEL & GLASS

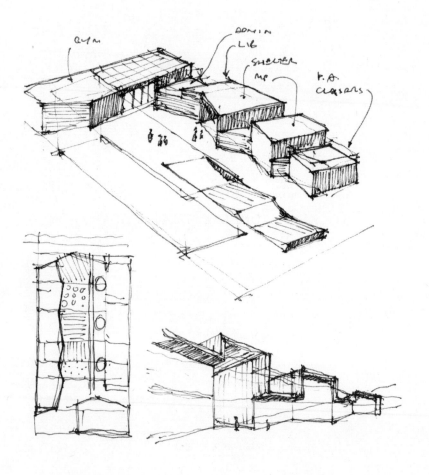

Sunset over Hermosa Beach

I can't do what ten people tell me to do.
So I guess I'll remain the same.
OTIS REDDING AND STEVE CROPPER

WE WON THE competition—three times. And we lost—three times!

The three-year affair known as the Hermosa Beach Pier design competition of the early nineties was mostly a hard lesson in personal naïveté, civic dithering, and professional backstabbing. The sunny part of it, however, was that it enabled my design partner and me to engage in an aspect of architecture—public space—that is not discussed as passionately as are tangible exhilarating structures of steel and glass.

Public space is architecture that is shared by all who encounter it directly or who live or work nearby, not just by the inhabitants of a home or office. An individual, a group, a community—they all share and flourish in a public space, no matter how small. I'm not talking just about the great parks of the world, the lungs and soul of any city; they are of course essential to people of all means to spend an afternoon surrounded by trees and grass, away from concrete and noise.

I'm obsessed with plazas, vest-pocket parks, and expanded thoroughfares that give us five, ten, thirty minutes of respite. Even passing by a well-designed urban oasis can calm or energize us. To open up, look up, look around . . . before rushing on to the next destination.

For my early architectural studies, I conducted year-long research into the public square that defined my growing up: San Francisco's Portsmouth Square. Often called the "Heart of Chinatown," it shaped how I look at a city and at how people gather within it.

Portsmouth Square was carved out of the dense urban environment of Chinatown's old buildings. As a child, I climbed its play equipment; as a youth, I met my friends there after hours; as an adult, I celebrated my wedding there. Imagine my wife's bright white silk wedding dress against the gritty and grainy city backdrop, people on aged benches staring at us with curiosity, and the old men playing chess, not missing a strategic move, undistracted by a wedding party in tuxedos and gowns. Years later, my children would play in the same recreational areas of that venerable public space.

My photographs of Portsmouth Square went on exhibit at UC Berkeley and were later included in a book titled *People Places: Design Guidelines for Urban Open Spaces.* That vital public park imprinted on me. And it has informed much of my career's work.

As I backpacked through Europe during college, the piazzas, church squares, and gardens struck me collectively as an elemental form of architecture. I expected it, truth be told, but in the Piazza del Campo in Siena, I witnessed a civic jam session: children playing impromptu sports, groups dancing to live music, raucous political debates, benchlong napping, art students hocking their colorful creations, and one *very* romantic couple—and then me, the tourist and student in awe of how all this came together.

The final composition of a public space should boom with the splendor of a city performing on stage for the world to witness. As a city-scale work of cultural and social art, a public space and the activities within it are an expression of a community that is alive.

 SOUTHERN CALIFORNIA IN 1992. Economic times were tough, but the sun always shone. We were young, Greg Lombardi and I. I was twenty-eight and he thirty.

We formed a partnership, but we didn't go the artificial acronym route fancied by our colleagues. For us, there would be no OMA (Office for Metropolitan Architecture), FOA (Foreign Office Architects), or the illustrious Office dA (de, as in from Architecture?) in Boston. Our fancy name? Lombardi/Poon Associates.

Years later, when we obtained our state licenses as architects, we became—this is clever—Lombardi/Poon Architects. Rather than spend money on printed and embossed business cards, we ordered a fifteen-dollar custom rubber stamp and hand stamped our company's name onto precut card stock.

We were both trapped in miserable jobs: I as a paralegal temp and Greg as a corporate monkey at Universal Studios in Hollywood. We met in the evenings and on the weekends to plan and to sketch, just to keep our creative juices flowing.

We decided to enter a design competition organized by The American Institute of Architects for the redesign of the pier and waterfront of Hermosa Beach, one of the Los Angeles beach towns made famous by surf movies and volleyball tournaments: Hermosa, Manhattan, and Redondo Beaches, the cedar-shingled, salty cousins south of Santa Monica and Venice Beach. The trio of towns was and still is a string of funky pearls along the sweet curve of Santa Monica Bay.

Southern California loves its piers, and the piers here last longer than they do on the rest of the Pacific Coast or the East Coast. They aren't lashed as often by major storms, and a long, sloping shelf receives and holds the concrete pilings. Hermosa's pier, like the pier in every other beach town, was a place to fish and drink, or just do nothing. Piers are potent symbols of civic pride. We don't build *up* so much here; we often build *out*.

The competition was stiff, with some of the biggest names in Southern California as well as many international entrants in the running. Leading the group of jurors for the competition was teacher, practitioner, and community and industry leader Charles Moore, recipient of the 1991 Gold Medal from The American Institute of Architects. His 1978 Piazza d'Italia in New Orleans had captured worldwide attention and earned him a reputation as one of the original voices of Postmodernism.

The mighty local design studios of Morphosis and Eric Owen Moss Architects were believed to be the frontrunners. Greg and I would be the minnows.

Our design strategy was to consider the waterfront, the plaza at the foot of the pier, and the surrounding beach area as a blank canvas for a broad public space. Our philosophy was that the redesign should be a backdrop for the many activities of visitors to the beach: the bicyclists, the volleyball players, the families looking for recreation, the couples on a romantic stroll down the longest pier on the West Coast. In contrast to our competitors, who proposed hotels, shopping centers, and other large buildings, we ambitiously and simply proposed public space.

A slight tilt in our plaza design created long steps down to the sand, offering access to the beach while forming an amphitheater from which to watch the sun set. We envisioned a sweeping 250-foot elliptical shape carved out of the plaza leading up to the lifeguard tower, which would provide casual seating and organized traffic. We eschewed a focus on the retail shops; instead we added trees, wide sidewalks, benches and chairs. Public amenities.

Open space, taking advantage of the already beautiful surroundings. Public space.

 WE PRESENTED OUR scheme on four thirty- by forty-inch boards in an unusual manner. Rather than the expected architectural drawings, models, and computer renderings, we made heavily textured collages of colored paper, magazine clippings, and newspaper scraps. Our architects' statements were printed like fortune-cookie papers, red on white. Our montages were sandwiched between a clear sheet of acrylic on top and a blue piece of acrylic on the back. The blue acrylic glowed like California sky and Pacific Ocean water when light hit it.

We thought it was magical, beautiful. This aesthetic technique was innovative but also risky. Would the jurors appreciate our concept and presentation style, or would they not even understand our unconventional approach?

Our mantra for this project: People and nature have defined the design, not the architects. With this thesis, we submitted our long-shot, upstart entry into a big-time, big-name, international design competition.

We ended up winning, and then losing and winning subsequent rounds of voting and revoting. It's a saga not for this moment, but I did learn that my architecture road was going to be a long one—a competitive, creative, maddening, and soul-fulfilling one.

I never lost my affection for public space, for architecture that is for everyone, including a little kid on a swing, or a kissing couple, or chess players.

part one

ARCHITECTURE FOR GOOD

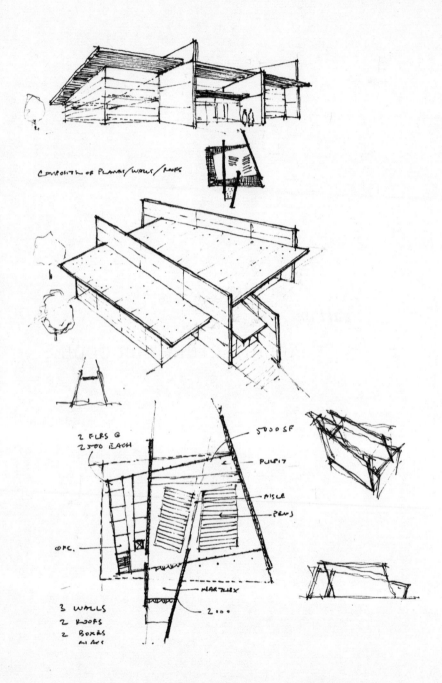

COMPOSITE OF PLANES/WALLS/ROOFS

2 FLRS @
2500 EACH

5000 SF

PULPIT

AISLE

PEWS

OFC.

MARBLEX

2000

3 WALLS
2 ROOFS
2 BOXES
GLASS

BLASPHEMY

*Nothing requires the architect's care more than the
due proportions of buildings.*

VITRUVIUS

GREG AND I were midlevel architects on a Seattle
firm's design teams working on gargantuan architecture for sports and entertainment: football and soccer
stadiums, basketball and hockey arenas, venues for performing arts and campus sports. For this firm, Greg and
I even submitted a proposal for the main arena for the
2000 Summer Olympics in Sydney, Australia.

Young and newly certified to practice, we were
working on large-scale structures that many people
would see, enter, and enjoy. For our age, we were fortunate to have influential roles in the Los Angeles sat-
ellite office.

After earlier stints where I had primarily designed
custom residences, this shift to sports buildings was

startling and thrilling. From designing structures for a family of three or four, I jumped to designing stadiums for thousands and thousands of spectators. Some large homes I laid out consumed twenty-five thousand square feet; a big-city sports arena complex can occupy over one million square feet. That's a 4,000 percent shift in scale and material.

Perhaps because the Seattle partners in the firm wanted the high-profile pro league or major university work seen through their West Coast myopia, I lucked into a small Midwest college project that would become "mine."

My assignment for the next three years would be a 400,000-square-foot convocation center for Xavier University in Cincinnati, Ohio. The new building would contain a 10,000-seat basketball arena, a 30,000-square-foot conference center, a 700-seat banquet hall, a 500-seat dining hall, and supporting kitchens, offices, locker rooms, restrooms, storage and mechanical spaces, and all that a complex like that entails. Brand-new, blank slate, ground up. Mine to do.

Projects like this are typically staffed with a principal-in-charge (the executive team leader), a project manager (the seasoned architect), and a group of architects led by the creative efforts of a project designer. At the modest age of thirty-two, many years ahead of my career schedule, I was named project designer.

Yes, me.

And even though I wasn't licensed in Ohio, architects without a license can practice if the firm they are with has licenses, so I was able to work in Ohio and later in Illinois in collaboration with a local firm.

THE LEADERS OF Xavier University warmly greeted us at the campus kick-off meeting. I dutifully followed in my place behind the leaders of the firm, as was proper. They would set the overall project goals, and I was to design it, and despite my cockiness, I was petrified. This wasn't a ten-hour architectural licensing exam; this wasn't a pier in a beach town, or a house. Small college or not, this was a *big* deal, for them and for me.

The principal-in-charge had bigger fish to fry, as he led architectural teams for NFL and NBA projects. A mere collegiate project couldn't keep his interest. Then, in the first month of the project, the bean counters back in our West Coast office determined that the architectural fee being paid by Xavier didn't cover the cost of the number-two person on the job, the project manager.

So I was left standing. One architect to do the work of three.

Limited experience.

Limited management resources.

What I did possess was determination. I was smart enough to figure things out as they came to me and dumb enough not to know when to be intimidated and scared. With no intention of becoming the road kill of corporate fallout and politics, I proceeded with keen ambition and irrational courage.

Every other week for over two years, Delta Airlines delivered me to Cincinnati, where I marched onto the Xavier campus accompanied by one supporting colleague. I ran meetings of dozens of campus leaders from seemingly every department and office: from the religious leaders of the campus to staffers in finance, athletics, administration, and facilities to alumni. Again, my ego and stupidity sheltered me from the fact that I should have been worried.

Though the job was overwhelming, my self-esteem ran high. I'm sure many in attendance at the campus meetings asked themselves, "Who is this youngster architect?" But with the rehearsed bravado in my presentations, I bulled my way through, undaunted.

The Cintas Center was ambitious and monumental and is still the largest building on Xavier's campus. I dubbed my vision "a city within a city." Many projects that propose new buildings near established sites involve having to build nearby but not within the institution's current boundaries. Existing campuses, be they colleges, hospitals, or apartment complexes require either razing older structures or building *out*, in a parking lot or on a plot annexed across a street or stream. Before I visited Xavier, founded in 1831, I assumed that would be the case, that the land within the ancient walls would already be taken.

But the university fathers had vision, and several open areas on campus were available to me. Since I wasn't to build on an outlying lot across from the campus, with few obstacles other than existing roads, I was forced to be more creative, more aware of the need for the project to blend into the campus. A city within a city.

I placed the Cintas Center in the heart of campus, tucking it against an eighty-foot-high hillside. This location served both an aesthetic and a practical purpose. The hillside as backdrop served to diminish the new center's overwhelming size, and it allowed the arena to be entered from several levels at the top, middle, and bottom of the hill, easing the flow of ten thousand fans arriving at one time.

One of my favorite concepts for this project was to brand the building, to make it into its own sign. I chose to carve the school's logotype into the massive fifteen-foot-tall, forty-five-foot-wide precast concrete panels of the exterior. Starting on one side and turning the corner, XAVIER, in eight-story-tall letters, was to be emblazoned permanently. And I'm proud to say that, although it was at first controversial, this design element is now an icon of the campus and the avatar of the Cintas Center's Twitter feed.

But I had to sell the idea to a tough group.

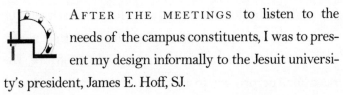 AFTER THE MEETINGS to listen to the needs of the campus constituents, I was to present my design informally to the Jesuit university's president, James E. Hoff, SJ.

"Informally," I was told by the president's handlers. "Don't worry," they assured me. I didn't know then that "Don't worry" meant the opposite. I was still the young architect, eager to please and impress, and I usually took people at their word.

I sauntered into the administration building thinking I would be sitting in the cozy, historic president's office on a comfy burgundy leather club chair, the president and I talking one-on-one. I imagined a delightfully intellectual conversation about buildings, education, young people, the past and future.

Instead, I was directed into a large, very formal chamber, a daunting dark-wood-paneled room that clearly represented the powers and traditions that had led the college for over 150 years. As I walked in, feeling like a cat ready to run at the first sign of trouble, a long table was getting fresh white linens. A huge floral arrangement dominated a side table on which steam trays, plates, and silverware were laid out. Above it hung a giant blue banner with the university's seal in Latin, *Vidit Mirabilia Magna*, which I would learn later translates to "He has seen great wonders." A dozen waiters stood along one wall in starched black-and-white uniforms.

To top it off, the president's crest was being hung on the wall behind his high-backed chair.

This was no "informal" meeting. This was possibly the most formal setting in which I had ever presented. The lesson: There is no such thing as an informal meeting with a president.

I remained calm. My ego, my shield, protected me. As I unpacked and arranged my presentation in the middle of one long side of the table, the university's leaders walked in, each in full black Jesuit garb. Fortunately, I had arrived early enough to set up a building model on the long table and cover it with a white cloth. Architectural presentation needs an element of theater, I had learned early on.

After each university leader arrived at his or her

assigned chair around the table, President Hoff, in a black cassock and white collar, was quietly but dramatically ushered in; there's theater in entering a room as well, it turns out. Settling in, they all stared at me, wondering when the architects, plural, were going to show up.

Without hesitation, I stood up and spun my vision about creating "a city within a city" for Xavier University. I spoke passionately about how their existing Collegiate Gothic style of architecture need *not* be formulaically followed in the design of the new Cintas Center. I held up my presentation boards in a calm and orderly manner, and then, like a magician—or was it a bullfighter?—I unveiled the miniaturized but, I thought, still impressive model of my design for the center.

Silence.

When I lifted off the roof of my model to reveal the basketball arena within, there were gasps. Literally. I couldn't tell yet if they were from shock or delight.

As I wound down my comments, the leaders of the school wound up. Many questions were thrown my way, which is how it should be—a rational exchange, a give-and-take—but the volume and depth of inquiry were quite impressive, no doubt coming from a well of concern for their institution and concern about the too-young architect of a dramatic proposal for their home turf. The questions were politely put at first, but the heat continued to rise, among themselves and against me.

Besides questions about budget, construction, schedule, engineering, and permits, the main point of dispute was my aggressive proposal to reinterpret the proud Collegiate Gothic style represented by every other building on campus into a composition of clean modern lines and massive concrete forms. A consensus arose in the room not only that my idea should be revisited but that I, this solo architect from a big company out West, should be reconsidered.

I think I actually heard someone whisper not so quietly, "Blasphemy."

Despite the impressive physical model, with its "concrete" walls and its little cars painstakingly glued in carefully measured spaces, there were no heads nodding in support of my vision, particularly not for my bold idea to deboss the giant letters of "Xavier" on the building's facade.

I shrank against the onslaught. My vision of a grand structure turned into the image of an Asian kid surrounded by venerable white men in robes. Curiously, one even questioned, "Does he really speak English?" I was not only a bad architect; some in the room saw me as a blasphemous circus act speaking in tongues.

I had about ten seconds to think of something, anything, or be chased out of this hallowed room. Although I was sweating, I calmly declared, "This project is not about the past. This project looks toward the future. Gothic architecture is from centuries ago, and I envision a new world, a new future, and a new city within a city for Xavier University!"

Everyone gulped, then, one by one, turned their heads to the president for direction. The silence seemed to last a century of Xavier history.

President Hoff said steadily, "I like the words that you are saying, young man!"

And with that, the room broke into excitement and applause. The meal began. Wine was poured.

With a mere gesture of approval from the president's hand alongside his direct and simple words, I was now a hero, a creative force to be reckoned with. My head couldn't have grown bigger, and my ego could not have been more stroked.

The project opened in 1999 to accolades and national attention. In the arena of my design, in "my house," the Xavier Musketeers regularly crushed competitors, distinguishing themselves as one of the country's premiere college basketball programs.

At the groundbreaking, President James E. Hoff, SJ,

released a statement: "When the Cintas Center is finally finished, we will continue to look back on Anthony Poon's work with the highest regard. It was a pleasure for Xavier University to work with Anthony."

Later President Hoff asked me to step out with him for a brief note.

"Yes, Mr. President?" I asked curiously.

He asked me to call him "Jim."

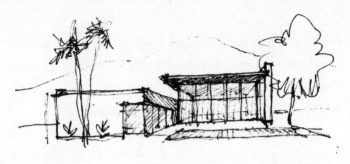

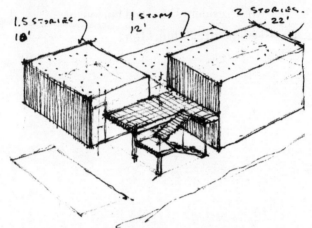

1.5 STORIES
18'

1 STORY
12'

2 STORIES.
22'

CHINESE THEMES · BIG SCALE
RE-INTERPRET'D
ELEMENTAL MATERIALS
ASIAN MODERN

OF CRAFT
VOLUME, HANDCRAFTED
SCALE, DUMPLING, AGGREGATE
SMALL THINGS
EXQUISITE
SOMETHING SPECIAL

2/19/13 MAU
CUBE SCHEME

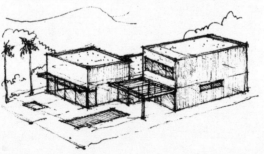

MODERN FOR THE MASSES

Our greatest responsibility is not to be
pencils of the past.

ROBERT STERN

Is IT POSSIBLE to design and build affordable, "green,"
and exceptional single-family housing in an age of cookie-cutter housing and bottom-line developers? It turns
out the answer is yes. With creativity, luck, and an exciting vision, "production housing," also known as tract
housing, can be cool, modern, and luxurious, even for the
masses.

Ever since humankind transitioned from a nomadic
life to clustered settlements, families have yearned for
free-standing solid structures composed of local materials. Most often shelters went up alongside similar structures for reasons of cost and availability of building
blocks, be they mud, clay, brick, thatch, or wood. With
time and resources, the same yearning stretched toward
the creation of unique family homes, a way to stand out

and signal prosperity. As the centuries cycled through population growth and economic swings, we found our way back to the need for mass-produced homes that could go up quickly and efficiently. We have seen this in several waves in the United States over the past seventy years alone.

We are all familiar with the post–World War II housing boom. William Levitt & Sons built new towns for returning GIs and their families seemingly overnight on rich farmland and in pine forests east of New York City and along the East Coast. These communities consisted of houses that were identical save for the paint color. In short order, Americans burst their way south and west. Single-family homes went up in quick succession from Florida to California, on marsh and desert as well as farmland. That this second wave was almost too big for the banks to handle, and that these were the homes purchased and lost in the recent mortgage bubble, doesn't change the ever-present demand for affordable single-family homes, each with the moat of a lawn. Trees optional.

While we have all seen firsthand or in photos and movies the seeming sameness of row upon row of identical homes in America's blossoming suburbs, buyers still had the option to choose from a menu of interior variations, entry features, and other simple ways to put a personal stamp on their home. The same is true of prefab homes that we see off the highway, or in halves *on* the highway trailered behind a semitruck.

This type of tract housing is based on the concept of prototypes. An architect would design four prototypical designs for a community of a hundred homes. These prototypes would have variations and upgrades, such as a swimming pool, an extra bedroom, a sound system, a security system, or fancier cabinetry. The prototypes would come in a few exterior colors and landscape choices. Along with other facade options like an arch, a trellis, or a porch, the completed community would *not* look like a tract of the same four homes repeated monotonously; rather, you could get three to four dozen different-looking homes. Sort of.

For Poon Design, this industry of production housing was a new kind of client, a different kind of business, and an entirely distinctive kind of architecture. The architectural team at Poon Design was vastly experienced with custom homes from the West Coast to the East Coast as well as in the south of France. These projects contrasted in every way with the premise of production homes.

We were limited as experts in speculative homes where the buyer was only a hypothetical idea. In our usual projects, a client hired us and we designed a single, special custom home. In addition, the custom homes we designed were larger, were more complex, and had a bigger budget than was typically seen in the production housing industry. As an example, a production home might sell for $400,000 to $800,000, on average, in the areas where we were to work. The custom homes that we designed sold for $2 million to $100 million. Production homes are affordable, average-sized homes, often for a first-time or retired buyer, or perhaps for someone purchasing a weekend home.

When developer Andrew Adler, CEO of Alta Verde Group of Beverly Hills, approached us with a vision for modern production housing, we found the challenge presented by this new client fascinating and the philosophical goals worthwhile. Poon Design was interested in honing our exclusive design talents to provide sensational visionary homes for the mainstream U.S. home buyer. We wanted to find ways to distill and translate good design for an industry of prototypes, repetition, mass production, fast construction schedules, and economical budgets. After decades of designing expensive homes for the wealthy, we strongly believed in creating an approach that would offer creative concepts and great design to everyone.

For a client paying us to construct a custom home, a budget of $1,000 per square foot would be considered typical, though extravagant for many. It is not difficult to execute a nice estate with such a generous budget. When a developer suggests that his production homes are to be constructed for one-tenth that amount—$100 per square foot—our most creative skills must come into play. How do we achieve results similar to a custom residence for a fraction of the amount?

Though we had the advantage of saving money in construction due to building in volume with production housing, we still needed a host of creative and strategic ideas. Building a dozen homes at one time, as compared to a single home, would no doubt offer discounts in construction labor and materials, but a volume discount alone would not create the enormous savings that our developer client needed.

A house is a home, and everyone should have a chance to own one, if that is their desire. Even the predictable traditional developers endeavored to artificially mirror local tastes, from clay tile roofs in the Southwest to gabled windows reminiscent of a perceived New England tradition. We were eager to meet the challenge.

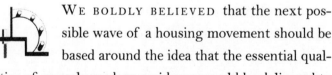 WE BOLDLY BELIEVED that the next possible wave of a housing movement should be based around the idea that the essential qualities of upscale modern residences could be delivered to the mainstream marketplace at affordable prices.

In truth, for me, it all simply started at a party.

One evening after work in early 2008, Poon Design

was hosting an informal office party for friends and colleagues to show off our expanded office space and new graphic design studio. We left our doors open to easily greet visitors.

A new neighbor had just moved into the adjacent office suite. As he was leaving his office, he heard our music, saw food, drinks, and a group of people enjoying themselves, and wandered in to introduce himself.

Andrew Adler looked around our studio, examined the giant glossy prints of our projects, studied our conference room with a presentation from earlier in the day and work areas littered with remnants of the week's creative process, and talked to a few architects in the room.

Adler found me and said, "We could do great projects together, and we should talk."

Adler and his newly formed residential development company, Alta Verde Group, had exciting ideas. He had previously developed successful urban infill condominiums and apartments in Texas, garnishing a myriad of accolades for breaking boundaries in housing design and urban development. He had just relocated to build and sell residential homes in Southern California after the real estate crash of 2007.

The country's economy was slipping fast into a recession, and distressed land was available at reasonable prices to purchase and develop. In some cases, such land was already destined for detailed communities, with roads, sewer, and electrical lines already in place to service surveyed plats awaiting beautiful new homes. The business model was for a developer to build the homes at his or her risk, with the intention to sell them at a profit. In most cases, this common speculative plan was successful, but in an economic downturn, many developers' plans went unrealized. The land remained vacant, and cleared land was selling at bargain prices.

Alta Verde was looking to buy this land and construct homes, but with an all-new, innovative approach. Adler envisioned cutting-edge design, unique but affordable materials, and yes, environmentally conscious structures. He imagined clean lines, uninterrupted glass walls, and dramatic interior spaces—all on a budget. Adler saw in the work on our walls a sympathetic creative partner in Poon Design. In our custom-built residences, he could see our desire to do things differently—to accommodate while engaging an artistic process.

We knew that with so much cool, advanced, and affordable design in every device from cars to laptops, the new generation of home buyers would expect the same in their homes, but at reasonable prices, especially in California.

For the Alta Verde project, we banned the words "prefab" or "tract home" from our lexicon; those words simply would not fly with our client.

Our vision was to bring the essential elements of

good design—proportion, light, scale, space, authenticity, and flexibility—and apply advances in smart technology, sustainability, and new materials. We wanted to be at the forefront of a new chapter in California modern design. Adler and I were in agreement as to what would be allowed and what would be eliminated from the design dialogue. No Mediterranean-Spanish-inspired stucco boxes for us. No overly thick faux-adobe walls, with small windows that limit a connection to the California landscape. No inefficient, costly, and heavy clay tile roofs, and no wedding-cake-style decor of plaster that lacks authentic beauty or inherent visual detail.

We also believed that a key aspect of great residential architecture was no longer about the one-off experimental custom homes that show up on the covers of magazines. We believed, and still do, that today's home design should not focus on creating a singular architectural jewel for one family to enjoy; the higher value and impact of good architecture can happen on a community scale.

That was all well and good. We were ready to dive in. But the real challenge to our concept? Cost per square foot. Large budgets make marble and grand staircases de rigueur; Adler challenged us to adjust our creativity to what he called "democratizing good design."

This concept is not new. Michael Graves famously adapted his original high-end Postmodern tea kettle into an accessible and stylish item for Target. Graves had first designed his famous colorful kettle years previously for Alessi, an Italian kitchen-utensil distributor that represented some of the most well-known architects and designers of the time, such as Ettore Sottsass, Philippe Starck, and Zaha Hadid. Many of Alessi's products are so celebrated that they are exhibited in the permanent collections of museums around the globe, including MoMA in New York City.

The tea kettle Graves designed for Alessi was priced at several hundred dollars for the cooking-obsessed collectors of exquisite design. The Target kettle was nearly exactly the same in concept, aesthetic, and details. The delightful vision of Graves's design, originally available only to the wealthy, became accessible to the average shopper at Target, who, though shopping on a budget, still sought original, smart design.

Andrew Adler had the same thought about homes. The only hurdle now was financing.

 FOR ADLER AND his Alta Verde Group to present the idea of a new class of homes and find investors, they needed developed architectural ideas, graphics, and presentations to show off in the pitch. With the real estate capital market having a hangover from the recent crash, locating leverage for construction was going to be a challenge, and even more so for modern homes in a conventional marketplace. Alta Verde had to create their capital program in stages and was not yet prepared to hire us as their full-time architecture company to design these homes in detail. But I felt this opportunity for exploration would reap great rewards, both in exposure and in personal merit.

With some risk, we agreed to provide one year of free design service in exchange for securing the future contracts to execute the projects. We would create a repertoire of architectural designs to entice investors. If Alta Verde was successful in finding the appropriate project funds, Poon Design would land a full plate of exciting new work. The bet on the vision and the players was made.

From 2009 to 2010, Poon Design planned groundbreaking homes that were starkly modern, open and sleek, and also welcoming and timeless; the last two adjectives are typically used to describe a successful house design.

Month after month after month, toiling late at night in eight-hour nonstop design sessions totaling hundreds, even thousands, of hours, Adler and I dedicated ourselves to a journey toward the unattainable ideals of creative perfection. Complementing my architectural skills, Adler brought his own design talents, an intuitive understanding of art and aesthetics, and his insights into emerging demographics. It was a remarkable and stimulating collaboration.

An upcoming chapter speaks to my training in classical music; with these homes, we composed structures in a relationship akin to a musical partnership. My design studio became an open workplace where Adler and I, alongside the architects at Poon Design, improvised and pioneered new ideas for a stale housing industry. Back and forth we drew, revealing our belief that shelter is more than a roof over one's head. Rather, it is also a form of art. We explored ideas of sculpture and composition, massing and scale.

We also investigated new ideas in infrastructure for lighting, mechanical, and plumbing systems as well as solar power. Our homes had expansive walls of glass and tall sliding doors for bright, airy interior spaces to connect to the outdoors. The public aspects of the homes—living room, dining room, and kitchen—were combined into one large, flexible, loft-like space with high ceilings and a sense of grandeur and luxury. We researched new materials, green ideas, landscape concepts, and construction methods that would be inventive to the market, fast to construct, and within a developer's budget. As for speed, a custom home can take years to build, whereas our type of production home was to take less than half a year.

Again, the homes had to be built for a *fraction* of the

cost of a custom home. We had to delve even deeper into the challenge of balancing quality with style by revisiting every building spec of a home. Instead of having multiple ceiling heights, as is common in a custom home, we limited our designs to two: eleven feet for the public spaces and nine feet for the private spaces (bedrooms and bathrooms). We also designed extremely efficient floor plans with no wasteful vestibules, niches, and hallways.

Not only did such straightforward, though not always obvious, approaches simplify the construction of the home and thereby save tremendous amounts of money, but the ideas delivered powerful, dramatic spaces of architecture. The design was not about crown moldings, vaulted ceilings, and arches; rather, the homes represented elemental aspects of architecture: light, proportion, scale, and space.

To save even more on costs, we found materials and finishes that were affordable but delivered the same sense of quality as is found in a luxury estate, such as porcelain floor tile in lieu of marble, textured precast concrete veneer in place of exterior limestone, or prefabricated cabinets of Italian high-finish laminates instead of custom wood or lacquered cabinets. We even created a new front-entry door concept, filling a fiberglass-shell door with concrete so as to affordably provide quality, security, and acoustic insulation. These ideas, alongside dozens more, delivered a high-end modern home at a budget previously considered impossible. We even planned to use prefabricated elements such as roof trusses that would be high in quality but save a tremendous amount of time and money.

 IN THE FIRST year of our design work, research, and development, we were designing without a physical site in mind since the developer had not yet purchased any properties. We planned in the abstract without a particular climate, orientation toward a particular view, specific topography, or solar direction. We were creating designs so potent in their simplicity that they were adaptable to any terrain, city, and general locale.

At the end of this first year, and after many presentations to potential investors, Alta Verde successfully landed a large capital commitment from an international investor and also obtained construction financing from two California lenders who embraced the Adler/Poon vision.

Things were about to move very quickly. Alta Verde's first deal was in Palm Springs at a development called Escena. In 2010 and 2011, Poon Design developed four home prototypes for 130 lots on 21 acres. All four of our prototypes were three-bedroom homes, between 2,200 and 2,600 square feet, fitting on an average lot size of just 7,200 square feet.

We utilized many of the ideas from our first year of research, which we then adapted and enhanced for this desert climate. These ideas included extended roof overhangs for passive cooling and protection from the heat, drought-tolerant native landscaping, and the use of regional building materials. The green home scheme provided the base design with a reflective, energy-efficient cool roof, electric-car charger setups, LED lighting, and a 2- to 6-kW rooftop solar array.

The media following the project coined it "Modern for the Masses," certainly a clever and appropriate moniker at the time. Danny Yee, our creative partner and graphic artist, dubbed the new kind of projects "This Century Modern," a nod to the ever-popular Midcentury Modern that signaled the first phase of a different building style in California and around the world. Danny's phrase acknowledged moving forward today and on toward the future.

At the time of this writing, nearly two hundred homes have been built and sold in just three years, and several new phases of presold home construction have begun. As intended, we delivered exclusive modern design to the general home-buying market at incredible value.

We transformed the production industry, raising it to

a caliber previously witnessed only in custom, multimillion-dollar homes. With our design success, we discovered a whole new demographic that sought our modern architecture. The buyers loved the Alta Verde homes, the media loved them, and a dozen national design award committees did as well, honoring all of us with "best in class" industry accolades for design excellence from organizations such as the National Association of Home Builders. Our design partnership with Andrew Adler and his belief in us had paid off.

A CLOSING NOTE on any innovative yet affordable residential architecture.

A colleague of mine revisited the Levittown homes of the 1940s for a piece published in the *New York Times* on the fiftieth anniversary of the once-groundbreaking mass-production tract homes. Regardless of some architectural embellishments added on by homeowners over the decades, he reported that he could still see the basic shape of every home, repeated house after house. This bothered him at first, but only briefly. It occurred to him that he was looking for the original design, and therefore he saw it and was pleased. But does this bother me?

Five-foot saplings were now fifty feet tall. That's fine.

But my colleague saw changes to the original designs: new coats of paint with a garage added here, a sun porch there, even some roofs raised to allow second floors.

In some cases, I feel that homes are as alive as the inhabitants. The architecture molds and gets broken in like a pair of jeans, to reflect the evolution of one's lifestyle. But on the other hand, I have witnessed, unfortunately too many times, the devastation of beautiful Midcentury homes by thoughtless remodels and additions in the seventies and eighties—just as one example.

Are my homes at Escena intended to be works of art, or do I now let them go into the untrained hands of the purchasers of my homes? What happens at a restaurant when a diner customer asks the Michelin-rated chef to substitute A-1 for his classic béarnaise sauce?

My ego, matched by the developer's, would like to see our Escena home designs remain pure. The homeowners, supporting the concept that they have purchased a work of art, have expressed little interest in adding their own brushstrokes of color to what are essentially pieces of modern art and sculpture.

To ensure our philosophy, we even added clauses to the sales contracts and community guidelines that prohibit architectural alterations. Sure, the landscape will change and grow, but certainly no second stories, added trellises and entry features, or guest-bedroom additions are allowed at our community.

Unlike many other residential developers who allow homeowners to choose from many options of paint colors, kitchen countertops, bathroom tiles, and so on, with Alta Verde Group, we decided that we produced the best compositions of residential design. If the home buyers do not like the model they see, they should consider looking at another one. If that doesn't work out, perhaps they should visit a competing developer's community. Our confidence has proven acceptable, as Alta Verde outsells all other developers in the region combined. Month after month.

No, I have not created Fallingwater or the Palace of Versailles, where such iconic designs are worth preserving forever. We have merely offered the newest ideas to an industry of production homes starving for fresh designs. But I do believe that in many cases, and perhaps in mine, that the original vision of an architect should be respected. The rest is up to history.

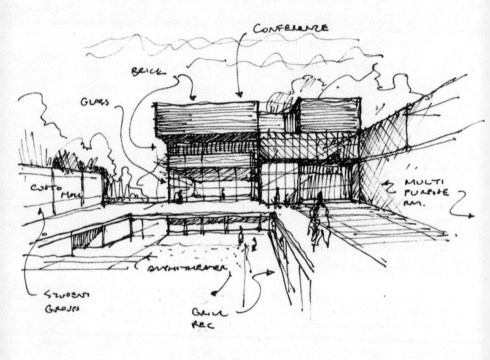

CONFERENCE

BRICK

GLASS

COMM MTG

MULTI PURPOSE RM.

AMPHITHEATER

STUDENT GROUPS

GRILL REC

GREENWASHING

*All the human and animal manure which the world
wastes, if returned to the land, instead of being thrown
into the sea, would suffice to nourish the world.*

VICTOR HUGO

SAVING THE PLANET has become an intense topic of popular and political debate. What you may not know is that for decades, the means to this end has been deceptively marketed to consumers, often to the detriment of the cause. The architecture and building industry has been as complicit as anyone.

Since the environmental movement of the '60s, and the founding in 1970 of both the first Earth Day and the EPA, most people have been aware of myriad things they could do to make the world an ecologically sounder place, from recycling to using unleaded gasoline. Madison Avenue has exploited our desire to do good—or to be seen as doing good.

In the 1980s, a researcher discovered that those ubiquitous tent cards in hotel bathrooms asking us to use the bath towels a second or third day were an attempt to *appear* environmentally conscious when the real intention was to increase profit by saving on hotel operating costs. (I also wonder if those cards cost more in nonrecycled card stock and non-petroleum-based ink than any possible operational savings.)

The term "greenwashing" was coined as a result and now applies to marketing attempts intended to deceive the public, to give products a "green sheen."

It got so bad that the Federal Trade Commission had to step in. Here is just one passage of the green guidelines set by the FTC: "Overstatement of environmental attribute: An environmental marketing claim should not be presented in a manner that overstates the environmental attribute or benefit, expressly or by implication. Marketers should avoid implications of significant environmental benefits if the benefit is in fact negligible."

In my world, there has been a concerted effort by the government to issue guidelines, incentives, and certification to architects and builders for "green" buildings. I am a LEED-accredited architect, meaning I have passed a lengthy and detailed test created by the U.S. Green Building Council (USGBC). On its website, the USGBC defines LEED as follows:

"LEED, or Leadership in Energy & Environmental Design, is transforming the way we think about how our buildings and communities are designed, constructed, maintained and operated across the globe. Comprehensive and flexible, LEED is a green building tool that addresses the entire building lifecycle recognizing best-in-class building strategies. At its core, LEED is a program that provides third-party verification of green buildings. Building projects satisfy prerequisites and earn points to achieve different levels of certification." The USGBC site goes on to list a point system for achieving silver, gold, or platinum LEED status for a building, with every possible aspect taken into consideration, from advanced cooling systems to ecofriendly building materials, from low-water-use landscaping to, yes, the ubiquitous solar panel.

In the best and sincerest way possible, I believe in being a steward for the environment, both the physical and the social. Aside from the exciting flights of artistic fancy in architectural design, architects are trained to provide, at a minimum, shelter that takes into consideration life, safety, security, and human welfare.

This broad and simple premise covers many subcategories such as aesthetics, budget, construction techniques, and material research. Specific to this discussion, I believe that practicing as a professional in the field of architecture means the responsible acknowledgment and handling of our environment, society, and culture for the next and succeeding generations. This position is a matter not just of ethics or virtue but also of common sense and decency.

Here's the catch.

Building "green" has become a necessary bragging right and sometimes a misleading marketing position to attract customers. Greenwashing can take the form of companies who change the names of their products to sound greener, add a green banner to their website, and then call themselves leaders in the green industry. Such companies spend more dollars in creating the spin and aura of being green than in bona fide research to support the supposed environmental benefits of their projects.

For example, some architectural products now sold as green are the same as their "pregreen" ancestors. Precast-concrete items are now marketed as "Enviro Sand Resin" or "Eco-Panels" that can achieve a "10-Point Green Premiere Certification of Carbon Neutrality and Reduced Emissions." This sounds great—except that the concrete-manufacturing company invented that ranking.

Another concrete company's website lists the LEED points its concrete can earn the builder, which is perfectly valid, but the site would benefit further from additional links to lighting, roofing, and other suppliers to fill in the bigger picture.

On the positive side, LEED standards really can lower the carbon footprint of a building. Still, most good architects were practicing green design before sustainability became an agenda.

I think of my friend Nicole, whose father was an architect in Australia. As an example of his green design, which he never labeled as such or cared to do so, he went to great lengths to limit or eliminate any construction material waste, which is one of the most basic foundations of being green. Every piece of wood was from a standard length of lumber or sheet of plywood off the shelf, not custom fabricated. Calculations in advance resulted in fewer waste pieces, and scraps were used down to the nub. Never discarded, remaining pieces of materials were all used creatively in his design.

Nicole's father possessed the incredible intelligence, meticulous planning, and painstaking attention of an architect who had patience and just believed this was the way things should be done. This architect did not call himself a green architect, did not have his logo printed in green on recycled paper with soy-based ink, and did not market his approach as better than anyone else's. For him, this was just professional architecture and common sense.

COMPETITION FOR PROJECTS has increased, and the commitment to being green has become integral to marketing. In recent years, most public projects dependent on state funds have required the architect to be LEED-accredited and the project to be LEED-certified, whether the client had an understanding of all the requirements or not. As an incentive, some jurisdictions offer an expedited permitting process to projects that are intended to be LEED-certified or meet the city-authored independent green standards.

Why am I concerned? This is all good, right?

The end result is good in terms of the heightened awareness of the benefits of green living—and yes, some truly more efficient buildings—but are they the best they can be, and is there a sincere desire to be green, or just to be seen as green? When we were designing a new preschool in California, some committee members asked, "How much does it cost to get the solar panels we need to get the LEED rating?"

The certification process of a building is like receiving a report card, where the building is scored by an authorized agent and provided a LEED rating based on site design, efficient water usage, energy conservation, responsible use of materials and resources, and quality of indoor air and light. The LEED design and certification are broad and comprehensive, not limited to how many solar panels fit on the roof.

I obtained my LEED Green Associate accreditation in 2009 because, at the time, clients wanted proof that their architect was green. LEED accreditation was the only legitimate national stamp of approval that clients understood.

The portfolio of our completed works that are sustainable, the performance ratings of our projects, and the recommendations of past clients were not as relevant or as convincing as seeing the four letters L-E-E-D after my name on my business cards. I could spend hours explaining how our work is inherently environmentally conscious—but instead I just point to the LEED after my name.

In fact, the remaining challenge in many cases is to explain why a LEED building would cost more to construct but save money over time. Every piece of a building can be greener—and more costly—beyond the myopia associated with solar panels. A countertop made of recycled glass and stone may not be cheaper, but its recycled content reuses materials that would otherwise be tossed out as trash. Part of green architecture is using local materials, not unlike the local farm-to-table approach. Shipping marble from Italy consumes a *lot* of energy.

We create charts that show how the costs are earned back over time. We don't greenwash; we are up front about every aspect that truly makes for a better, environmentally conscious building with a healthier environment for the people who use it. It is important to understand how a building impacts the environment, individuals, and communities now and in the future.

We all know how everything from hybrid cars to iPhones sucks up rare earth minerals and consumes vast amounts of energy to produce. I look forward to the day when green products are manufactured in a green manner, when the price of everyday green products will be affordable to all. Someday, the green-colored window cleaner will not be twice the price of the blue-colored window cleaner.

When I'm as good as my friend's father, I'll use every scrap of wood and glass with 0 percent waste.

When I stop getting asked, first thing, about solar panels.

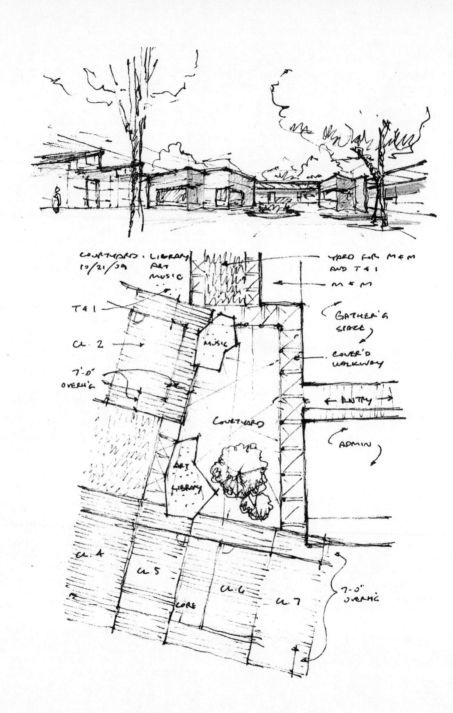

COURTYARD · LIBRARY ART MUSIC
10/21/09

YARD FOR M+M AND T+I

M+M

(GATHER'G SPACE)

COVER'D WALKWAY

T+I

CL. 2

7'-0" OVERH'G

MUSIC

← ENTRY →

COURTYARD

(ADMIN)

ART LIBRARY

CL. A

CL. 5

CORE

CL. 6

CL. 7

7'-0" OVERHG

ROOTS FOR THE UNROOTED

When we give cheerfully and accept gratefully,
everyone is blessed.

MAYA ANGELOU

A WORD ARCHITECTS overuse for all design is "vocabulary," i.e., the recognizable symbols we utilize to send overt *and* subliminal messages to both the inhabitants and passersby of any structure we design.

What about architecture for those truly in need, for those without a home? What kind of design would not just be serviceable but also provide a truly good and uplifting space for users?

For example, I delight in designing restaurants. To see one of "my" restaurants in action night after night, as an empty space fills with energy, is very rewarding. I set the stage for a vibrant social atmosphere, as well as for intimate moments, by shaping the bar and dining areas from floor to ceiling and then selecting just the right art, fabric, lighting, and materials. I apply the same attention to a client's new home or corporate headquarters. Grand gestures and clever details provide glamour and style. Such private projects are all well and good, but certainly, there is more to life. When my normally commercial work becomes a public service, then I feel I am a useful architect.

Twenty years ago, I was given a chance to design for good rather than for glamour. It changed my life.

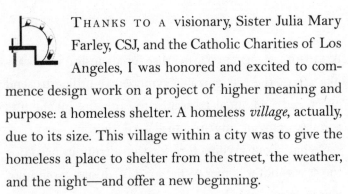 THANKS TO A visionary, Sister Julia Mary Farley, CSJ, and the Catholic Charities of Los Angeles, I was honored and excited to commence design work on a project of higher meaning and purpose: a homeless shelter. A homeless *village*, actually, due to its size. This village within a city was to give the homeless a place to shelter from the street, the weather, and the night—and offer a new beginning.

Rather than finding the perfect wood to panel a restaurant lounge or marble for a fireplace hearth, then working with a small design studio named KAA, we were to design budget-minded spaces and details that were just as warm and vibrant, even nourishing. The design, built in part from donated materials and partially constructed with volunteer labor, had to be affordable for a nonprofit organization and was also not to look utilitarian and coldly durable. We all know too well the depressing look and feel of a hospital hallway;

neither Sister Julia Mary Farley nor we wanted anything remotely close to that.

The three-part architectural program for the Good Shepherd Center for Homeless Women and Children proved groundbreaking. At the time, it was one of the most ambitious social housing projects of its kind. To label it a homeless shelter does not credit its larger mission: housing, rehabilitation, job training, and social re-integration.

Quite a challenge for a young architect.

The first area of the village consisted of transitional housing, residential rooms designed specifically for the homeless people who arrive straight off the street. The second area consisted of long-term apartments, serving the next step toward reentry into society for homeless women and children. The third area was diverse and commercial.

Alongside the apartments, we were asked to design a computer lab for job training, a career center, a youth center, and a social services department. There was also a commissary kitchen with a food service training program for residents employed at the public café on the grounds of the campus. This aspect of the master plan prepared the homeless population for productive placement back into the world through learning at the village, getting a job at the village, making money for themselves and for village operations, and eventually transferring the job skills to activities beyond the village.

Adding to this ambitious agenda, the structure also needed to promote use by disabled homeless women with children, another distinct aspect of the Good Shepherd Center. Supporting all of this, spiritually and managerially, our project also included a chapel and an administration building—a renovated Victorian-era mansion—on site.

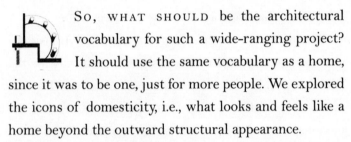 SO, WHAT SHOULD be the architectural vocabulary for such a wide-ranging project? It should use the same vocabulary as a home, since it was to be one, just for more people. We explored the icons of domesticity, i.e., what looks and feels like a home beyond the outward structural appearance.

To provide warmth and comfort, we employed such visual cues as the repeated gables that emanate from those of the Victorian-era mansion on the site. We chose a sloped roof rather than flat, factory-like building tops. While constrained by budget, we were still able to use appealing colors for the vinyl flooring, ceramic tile, and wall and ceiling paints. Door frames and windows were contemporary but not institutional.

The architectural challenge was not merely aesthetic, though the work was required to look good, even be appropriately beautiful. The goal was to use all of my architectural firm's skills but not to flaunt or boast.

We were to create something with value beyond steel, wood, and brick, beyond staying in budget and building on time, beyond allocating staff, resources, and overtime. The firm did not make a financial profit on this project, but that was not the point.

The compensation for such work came, and still comes, in being part of something noble and profound. Something inspirational. With deeper meaning to many.

 IN PREPARATION FOR this book, I revisited the Good Shepherd Center for Homeless Women and Children, twenty years on, to see how my design had lived up to expectations.

Upon entering the village of buildings, gardens, and playgrounds and then witnessing all the operations in full motion, I was moved. The place was alive with activity, and a sense of caring and humanity filled the air. Some rooms were being used differently than I had envisioned, but no matter; they were being used with good purpose. Though my own design skills have advanced greatly since that time, I am proud of this village. I am pleased to show off the good that architects and architecture can do.

As I walked with two of the heads of staff now running the facility, Adriana Sandoval and Annemarie Howse, they told me how much of an impact this village has made on its residents and also on the Los Angeles area. What began as a vision from an influential humanitarian and a sketch from an architect is now a fully working place of healing and regeneration. Especially enlightening for all of us was a chance to share our stories. Adriana and Annemarie were not present during the design process of the mid-'90s, so I provided them with a tour through our original thinking. I was not around during the years of implementation; they proudly gave me a tour of the realized, operational, thriving village.

The services provided through this 80,000-square-foot village currently assist over 1,000 women a year. Alongside the interior spaces for living and resting, the first-floor retail café where residents work and receive job training fairly hum. I was told that new tables and umbrellas were en route to shield the coffee and tea drinkers from the California sun.

I enjoyed seeing how, over the years, several decorators had volunteered their talents to provide warm interior design for the apartments. I helped create the larger canvas for the village, on which different artists and designers placed their signatures—a unique collaboration of many design minds working over decades, though never meeting.

Although I said earlier that the reward was in the work, not the recognition, I wasn't being completely honest. We were all absolutely thrilled when our design for the homeless village was honored with a design award from The American Institute of Architects.

I LEARNED A valuable lesson at the end of my tour with Adriana and Annemarie.

I met Sister Anne Lanh Tran, the center director, who has taken over the reins since the retirement of Sister Julia Mary Farley. In full collar and clerical cassock, Sister Anne quietly thanked me for my work and my visit. Then, with a theatrically raised eyebrow, she pointed out some water damage on the floor from recent rains.

"Over here," she pointed out to me, the architect.

All I had seen that day had already humbled me, and now I was made more aware than usual that there are daily amendments to an architect's initial vision, design, and construction. The inhabitants of any building, large or small, experience a building up close over decades, long after we've moved on to new projects. They see and are affected by whatever beauty we've created. But they also *experience* any imperfections.

"Let's have the contractor take a look at that," I replied.

A CIVIC GESTURE : ROOF

FUN PIECES : RAW SCHOOL

- ACADEMIES : DIFFERENT IDENTITIES

- ROOF REPRESENTS
  COMMUNITY
  CIVIC

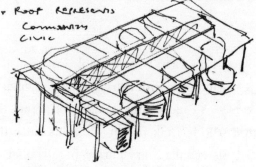

CLASSROOMS AND LEARNING ENVIRONMENTS
UNIFIED BY 'LEARNING IN ACTION'
ROOF. DYNAMIC. FOLDING. IN MOTION.

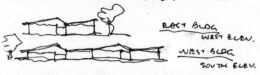

EAST BLDG
WEST ELEV.

WEST BLDG
SOUTH ELEV.

SPECIAL ED
WEST ELEV.

GABLE : RESIDENTIAL
INTERPRETED

DANCING ROOF

CLASSROOMS!
(1)

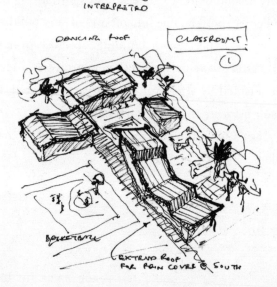

BASKETBALL

EXTEND ROOF
FOR RAIN COVER @ SOUTH

SCHOOL DISTRICT 129

The first thing that an architect must do is to sense that
every building you build is a world of its own, and that
this world of its own serves an institution.

LOUIS KAHN

WHILE YOU'VE PROBABLY noted that I am not a fan
of architectural firm abbreviations, a colleague and I allowed ourselves to create one out of enjoyment and purpose. Early in the new millennium, I launched a company with fellow architect Gaylaird Christopher. We called
our studio of a dozen architects A4E: Architecture for
Education.

Both a company name and mission statement, A4E
was committed to designing for the worlds of public
and private education: preschools and kindergartens; elementary, middle, and high schools; community colleges
and university buildings; adult learning centers. Serious
as our intentions were, we vowed to be imaginative and
even whimsical and child-like in our approach, down to
the logo on our business card—an abstraction of a classic yellow school bus.

Outside the home, a school is one of the first structured environments a child experiences. Our designs serve as the student's introduction to the outside world and also to his or her first civic duty. The belief in this engagement paved the way for us to shepherd a design process through critical interactions between us and teachers, students, administrators, staff, parents, and members of the community.

Two rare opportunities came through the doors of A4E in 2002. The first came via Gaylaird's lifetime of experience in school design and his work with Dr. Sherry Eagle, a prominent national educational leader and, at the time, superintendent of the West Aurora school district in Illinois. Currently, Dr. Eagle is the executive director of the Institute for Collaboration at Aurora University.

With an established trust and a new company that Gaylaird and I developed, Dr. Eagle selected A4E to create the architectural master plan for the entire public school district. Though modestly, almost generically, called "School District 129," or even just "SD129," this entity served over twelve thousand students from preschool to high school. The district passed a measure to spend a lot of money to deal with old schools and overcrowding; what exactly should the district do?

This job was a big deal for the town and for us.

A very big deal.

We conducted a six-month study of the entire West Aurora district: the condition of its current schools, land for new schools, parking and traffic patterns, student populations and growth, and proximities to parks—and especially educational methodologies that impacted our architectural thinking. As I had done during the Xavier University experience, we talked to *all* the constituents of the schools, notably teachers and administrators as well as parents and students.

We developed a master plan that was a road map, a strategic vision of what the future could become for the entire school district. It was a feasibility study based on a collection of site plans, floor-plan diagrams, budget spreadsheets, schedules, contacts, narratives, vision statements, and tons of community and user input. No fancy sketches of soaring windows and majestic breezeways—at least not yet. Just a strategic mission, and it was massive—and just a starting point.

At the end of this comprehensive effort, A4E concluded that the district could achieve its educational and community goals through the following building and renovation proposals: (a) one new elementary school with a preschool and university classrooms within, (b) one new middle school, (c) three additional buildings (gymnasium, music building, and a classroom wing) for the existing high school, (d) redesigns of the three existing middle schools, and (e) redesigns of the nine existing elementary schools. In total, eighteen connected, coordinated projects.

At first blush, you might not think this a radical plan. But consider the controversy over the High Line aerial greenway in New York City: $150 million was spent to repurpose a rail line, while many established parks were denied a mere $1,000 each to replace a few benches and play equipment. The High Line is one of the most inspiring architectural urban/public space concepts of our time. Politically and socially, however, its creation followed a predictable path of money spent with limited public input.

At SD129, we did the opposite. Our process was inclusive and democratic. The genius of Dr. Eagle's vision and of our master plan was to *not* invest in one humongous new showpiece of a high school to anchor the system and then just renovate the other buildings; she wanted *every* student and teacher in the district to benefit. One glorious new building stokes the ego and a career; a master plan that lifts an entire community stokes the imagination of every student and teacher within the schools' walls.

 SO, WHAT NEXT?

There were eighteen projects on the table for a public school district to support, approve, fund, and execute—trusting that two West Coast architects knew what they were doing. This was certainly not a modest proposal to spend public dollars on one singular gesture; it was a grand sweep of change, and one that Dr. Eagle, this school leader and visionary, supported completely.

Here is where the first opportunity of master planning segued into the extraordinary second opportunity for us—and the two were beautifully linked. After approval of our master plan, which in itself a feat, we went directly and astoundingly from master planning right into designing each and every building!

Typically, any master plan such as ours would have been doled out to several architecture companies to execute each project singly, which could also mean eighteen different city contracts and approval processes, and a lot of lost time. Time lost to us and to students who would benefit from the vibrant environments we had in mind.

In contrast to the usual course of events, SD129 retained A4E for *all* the projects under one contract. This Illinois city selected us, a California architecture studio, to design and implement *all eighteen projects.* They believed in us, and we believed in SD129's commitment to reenvision a whole educational community through architecture, to explore an entire educational methodology through design, and to go on a creative journey together.

As we established our master plan, then developed the architecture with participation from two local architects in the Chicago area, Cordogan Clark and Gilfillan/ Callahan—from statistics and urban diagrams to actual buildings, fields, and playgrounds—we held tight to our thesis that architecture should inspire education. Architecture should support education, not just be a physical facility or container to house students. It was this ambitious social agenda that separated us from regional and national competitors.

A4E originated architectural solutions that positively impacted education and the community. From color and pattern, materials and finishes, adaptable and flexible spaces, sounds and textures, natural light, and social spaces to student participation in the design process and to the overall concept of a school as an interactive, three-dimensional textbook, our architecture promoted curiosity, imagination, and wonder.

 THE A4E TEAM traveled once or twice a month to Aurora, a city known mainly as the hometown of the fictional *Wayne's World*. For two years, I rolled up my sleeves to design alongside educators, collaborate with local technical teams, assist the public construction bidding process, obtain approvals, present and receive endorsement from the Board of

Education, and ultimately watch over the construction process of all the schools.

The actual architecture of each project began by our meeting with each and every teacher to determine needs, expectations, ambitions, and dreams. Each group of educators had the power to influence the design of their own school from the mundane and utilitarian, such as ample storage and easy-to-clean flooring, to the bold and the ambitious, such as making a hallway itself the library, or a main staircase an amphitheater. Through this brainstorming journey, we built consensus and excitement; we generated ideas outside conventional architectural thinking.

Back home, alongside a staff of a dozen young architects in A4E's small studio in Old Town, Pasadena, I sketched, made physical models, and created presentations to be taken with great pride and anticipation to SD129.

Take the new Greenman Elementary School as an example. For this 62,000-square-foot school for 700 students, we generated architecture that focused on the school's interest in the performing arts. For example, the facade—a composition of glass, steel, brick, color, light, and shadow—is based on the notes and rhythms of J. S. Bach's Partita No. 2 in C minor. For the interior, we created a playful counterpoint of colored glass windows to provide visual interest and, more importantly, to offer a constant, thought-provoking view of the outside world for a young student.

Inside the building, sets of four classrooms were clustered into seven small communities. At the entry to each small "neighborhood," large wall murals were dedicated to different aspects of the performing arts: drama, dance, music, and so on. Here we enlisted help from the elementary school students, asking each of them to provide handmade drawings that represented their interest in the arts. I then took hundreds of these four-inch sketches and created half-a-dozen colorful and vivid mural-sized collages. The entries to each classroom cluster were transformed from the mundane into something dramatic, personal, and unique. The handprint of every student became part of the school.

The Greenman design also revealed the inner workings of a building. Whereas a building's mechanical room is typically considered merely functional and is hidden from view, our design displayed the area first-hand. We designed porthole windows at the landing of a staircase to reveal the building's heating and air-conditioning equipment and electrical panels at a child's eye level. Curious students now witness the hum, lights, meters, dials, and all the intriguing mechanics that power a school. Their school.

We accomplished these innovative design ideas,

among hundreds more, with a great deal of research and thought. We did it creatively and within the limited purse strings of traditional public funding. Our results had rarely before been seen for projects dependent on state dollars, which also needed to pass muster before public hearings and the Board of Education, plus city planning and building safety departments. My peers who specifically design private schools with substantially higher construction budgets could not believe that these buildings were designed with such imagination yet were also affordable. Our work was a model for other public school districts throughout the country.

All eighteen planned projects were completed between 2004 and 2006. In recognition of our architectural efforts, an unprecedented number of national honors and accolades were bestowed on A4E. We received design awards from the KnowledgeWorks Foundation, DesignShare, the Illinois Association of School Boards, the Illinois Association of School Administrators, the Illinois Association of School Business Officials, *School Planning and Management* magazine, and *American School and University* magazine. Our work was honored with the 2005 National Grand Prize, given jointly by Learning by Design, The American Institute of Architects, and the National School Boards Associations. Such an accolade is given to only one educational project in the country each year, and it was bestowed on our Greenman Elementary School design.

Better than the awards were these comments by those in charge of the schools and the students and teachers who would use them:

Greenman Elementary School is fantastic. It is beyond anything I imagined. I enjoy walking through the building every day remembering all the conversations with Anthony about his designs. I think about Anthony often and realize how lucky I was to be able to learn from him, about the concepts of design and education, and how important the two are when linked.

MS. ERIN SLATER,
Principal of Greenman Elementary School

School District 129 is fortunate to have Anthony Poon learn about us, and capture our spirit and beliefs about education in the buildings we will build for our children. I believe that Anthony's thinking and his work is extraordinary and will find its way to many honors. He will create the future dreams of this nation.

DR. SHERRY EAGLE,
former Superintendent of School District 129 in West Aurora, Illinois, and current Executive Director of the Institute for Collaboration at Aurora University

BACK TO OUR notion of being as child-like as possible in our enjoyment of A4E's work: The highlight of our visits to the schools after construction was to watch students and teachers delight in the movable walls and adaptable spaces for team teaching, a flexible wall that unexpectedly opened up the stage to the lobby, and the "secret" storage in the benches of the window bays. Students showed the teacher as often as the teacher showed the students.

Now, that's education.

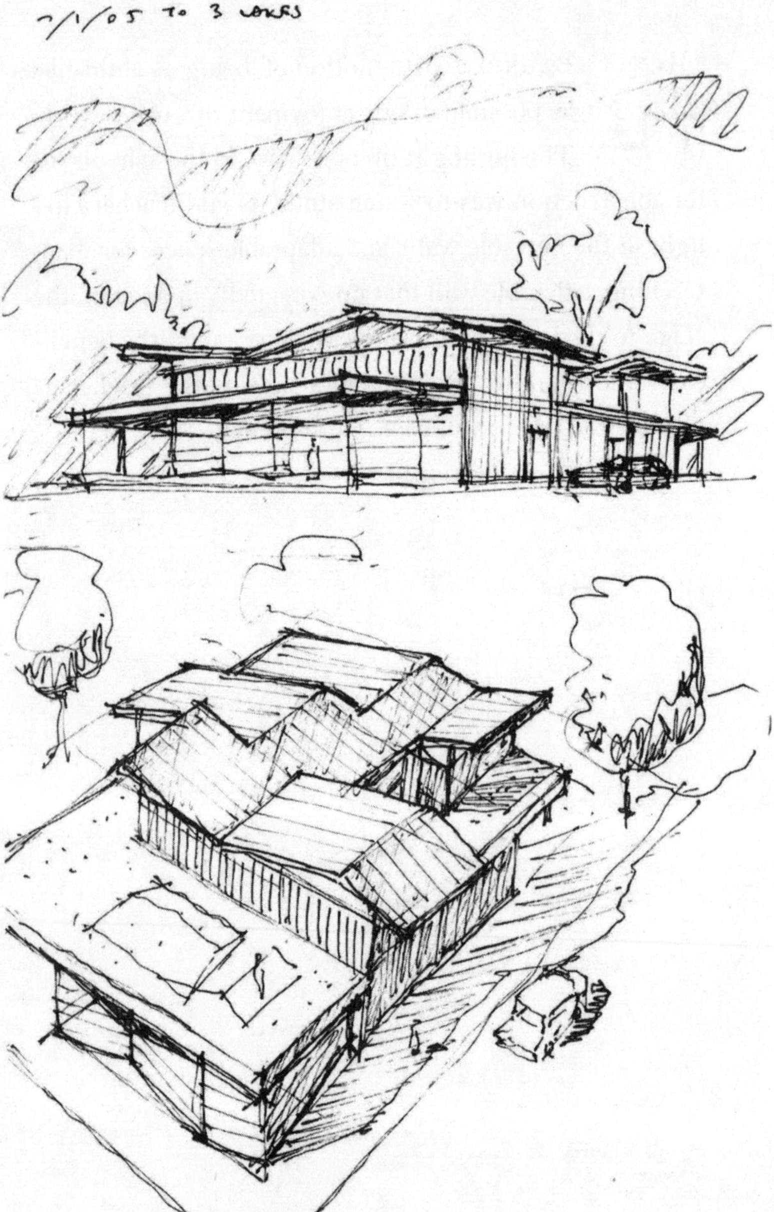
7/1/05 TO 3

LETTING THE SUN IN

We shape our buildings; thereafter they shape us.

WINSTON CHURCHILL

FOR ONE YEAR between moving my studio from Pasadena to Beverly Hills, I worked from my Hollywood Hills home with a panoramic city view. In an old-school, entrepreneurial way, my guest bedroom served as the offices of Poon Design.

I had four projects going: a 35,000-square-foot estate in Beverly Hills designed in collaboration with one of my mentors, David E. Martin; a yoga center in Santa Monica; the renovation of a Midcentury home in LA whose owner had found me by Googling "Architect, Los Angeles, Modernist."

Then came the real fun.

My fourth project fell under the category known as "mixed use"—a single complex or single building that mixes various functions, i.e., condos, offices, and retail. At the time, *new* mixed-use projects were uncommon; of course, many of the world's citizens live in apartments above a ground-floor store, but the new take on mixed use had the residents in the building more in mind, as well as environmental considerations.

I embarked on a project just south of Los Angeles in Manhattan Beach, a small coastal city. I titled this project the "WV Mixed-Use Project"; it was a mix of three condominiums, commercial street-level tenants, and underground parking all combined into one structure.

The letters W and V stood for the developer's name, which he wanted to keep private. When I created the project name, I thought the curious letters made the project sound hip and unusual. "What is WV?" many asked.

The two letters possessed interesting graphic qualities when pushed together. The waves of the letters, up and down, communicated the beach culture and ocean WaVes. Though those associations were admittedly clever and cute, you will soon hear more substantial ideas behind them.

Known as "design-build," the joint team of an architect (design) and a general contractor (build) would execute the WV project. Design-build is more and more common these days, though the majority of my work is still "design-bid-build." This simply means an architect designs the project first, then it is competitively bid by several general contractors, and finally the selected general contractor builds the architect's design. When structured strategically and properly, design-build can be an effective collaborative approach.

Networks and relationships drive a business, and perhaps drive life as well. Not short on coincidence, the WV project taught me that it is indeed a small world.

I met general contractor and design-builder Steve Lazar through his business partner Bryan Bethem, whom I met through Bryan's then girlfriend, now wife, Alicia Barnes, whom I hired when I was head of design at a sixty-person architecture company. Not long after I met Steve, Bryan joined Poon Design.

Steve reviewed my work carefully before we teamed up. A design proposal that I did for the 20,000-seat, 850,000-square-foot arena for the 2000 Olympics in Sydney, Australia, though never built, specifically impressed him.

 AFTER DEVELOPING THE design for this Manhattan Beach mixed-use project, we presented it to the city's Department of Planning and Zoning. The agency officials looked perplexed upon seeing a scheme with residential units next to, and even on top of, commercial spaces. Here was one of those cities that saw mixed use as peculiar, even brave.

"Why would someone want to live next to an office or a store?" probed the baffled city planners. Manhattan

Beach had residential neighborhoods, and the city had a downtown for businesses. The two functions did not come near each other, and specifically never in the same building.

This department stated that such a "one-of-a-kind" and "never-before-seen" project would have to go before the City Council for review. The project makeup was not that extraordinary in my mind, but each city has its own personality.

At a public hearing, we presented our project. Yes, indeed, we proposed several luxury condominiums adjacent to businesses, with the parking shared in an underground garage.

The council members were as puzzled as the city planners. Apparently only one other such project had been brought to the attention of the regulating agencies. This project happened to be in the works by KAA, the studio where I had designed both the homeless village in Los Angeles and the Nicole Miller flagship store in Florida (described in an upcoming chapter on fashion).

Believing that mixed use was a common concept everywhere, as it was in downtown Los Angeles, merely twenty miles north of Manhattan Beach, I spoke informally about our WV Mixed-Use Project, unaware that the council required a lesson in urban design and the history of cities.

The comments from the City Council that followed were amusing and frustrating.

"I never heard of such a thing: blending homes, offices, and stores?"

"I think I saw something like this in San Francisco. Or was it New York?"

"Hey, all of my fellow council members, *I* have traveled before. I went to Europe, and there, yes, it was there. I saw it. I saw *it*. I saw some retail at the street level, and families were living upstairs, right above the shops."

The hearing was surreal and entertaining, as if watching one of my kids learn to read: A, then B, then C. The City Council was not inane or senseless, just unfamiliar with what was already prevalent in cities throughout the world.

For hundreds of years.

Nonetheless, the ambition and spirit of the room rose. The council thought about the city's future and what developments would be fruitful. They were not stumped; they were just getting used to the idea of mixed use.

Unlike my experience with the adjacent city of Hermosa Beach, the oceanfront community of Manhattan Beach approved our WV Mixed-Use Project, *and* it was completed smoothly.

S<small>ITE CONSTRAINTS</small>, <small>AS</small> well as the interesting use of metaphors, drove my design for WV. The property was not large, though it had a high-profile corner lot, which was great for the developer's marketing and great for my design portfolio.

After slicing the site into several segments, as an urban planner would do with a London street of townhouses, I was concerned that not only was the massing of the building's composition dull and imposing but I needed to offer exterior spaces within this constricted site. Open green areas would be a great selling point for the condominiums.

Like playing with blocks or carving a chunk of clay, I pushed the "slices" forward and backward so that each condo would have an outdoor area. In one condo, this sunny area was to the side and the rear; for another condo, the grassy area was to the front; and for a third condo, the exterior patios were both front and back.

But—here is the big but. My potential landscaped areas were on the roof of the commercial space and portions of the ground-level residential units. We needed a design solution that allowed green space to be situated over commercial tenants. Instead of the typical inaccessible rock-covered flat roof, I envisioned gardens, berms, shrubs, even small trees growing out of the roof.

Some would say that our solution of the "green roof" is not a big deal—a sustainable roof design has been done many times. In the early 2000s, the ideal of a viable space beneath a planted roof was literally groundbreaking. The press recorded that Poon Design and Lazar Design/Build were the first to design, engineer, and complete such a roof in the South Bay of California.

In theory, a green roof was simple: a deep enough roof structure to hold soil, irrigation, drainage, and plant materials. In reality, a roof that can support the weight of trees in several feet of dirt, along with the irrigation pipes, water, and rainfall plus lighting, furniture, and a party of fifty people is a tremendous structural engineering feat. Don't forget waterproofing, acoustic insulation, vibration from the busy street, and even access for gardeners and their lawn-mowing equipment.

Through many discussions, research, and testing with the subcontractors and engineers, our design finally proved successful. As the perfect organic blank canvas, the condo owners could plant, shape, and garden as they saw fit.

Next challenge: How would I get natural light into each condo when they were to be squashed side by side? In sunny Southern California, particularly in a beach town, not capturing natural light in your living spaces is a design travesty.

This is where the metaphor comes in. Rather than a standard clay-tile gable roof or a factory-looking asphalted flat roof, I composed a roof of folding planes. With each tilt, the roof grabbed sunlight. The ups and downs of the roof allowed even the middle residential unit to have abundant daylight.

As noted with the graphic feel of the letters W and V, finding a metaphor for the beach culture, the recreational feel, the ocean waves, and the beach breezes fascinated me. I believed that my composition of folding roof forms articulated this culture. In turn, the architectural design became an aesthetic icon for this community that embraces its beach spirit.

UNLIKE MY SELF-RIGHTEOUS opinion that my Escena homes in Palm Springs are works of art that should forever remain as designed, the WV Mixed-Use Project has taken on the personal expression of the inhabitants.

And I like it.

The green roofs are fully planted, and for some, their space serves as a flexible lawn for entertaining. For others, it provides a personal garden space. The mangaris hardwood exterior planks and trim have aged gracefully, with the ocean's salty air casting a casual worn patina against the grain. It looks much better than the freshly stained wood we started with. A wide variety of furniture sits on the patios, the commercial spaces buzz with business activities, automobiles pull in and out of the parking structure, and colorful beach-cruiser bikes park out front.

The evolving state of "my" architecture tells me that this is not mine anymore. It is now a part of the urban fabric that ebbs and flows with changing lifestyles. Driving by each year, I witness how the owners have tweaked or added to the design to suit their needs and tastes. Some projects should be as alive and ever changing as the people within, yes?

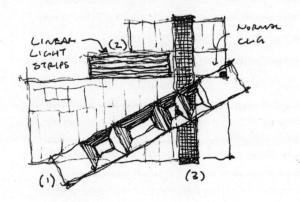

LINEAR LIGHT STRIPS

(2)

NORMAL CLG

(1)

(3)

(1) SPATIAL : VOLUME

(2) LIGHT : GLOW

(3) TEXTURE : MESH, DETAIL

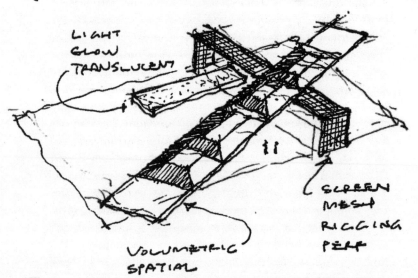

LIGHT GLOW TRANSLUCENT

VOLUMETRIC SPATIAL

SCREEN MESH RIGGING PERF

REMEMBRANCE AND
THE HUMAN SPIRIT

All my work is much more peaceful than I am.

MAYA LIN

THE JURY SELECTED Maya Lin, only twenty-one years of age, as winner of the design competition for the Vietnam Veterans Memorial in Washington, D.C. In 1981, this Yale University undergraduate triumphed over approximately 1,500 competitors that included national corporations, father figures in design, and some of the biggest innovators in architecture.

Lin's design immediately sparked artistic debates and fueled controversy about her youth, ethnicity, and gender. Rather than the typical memorial of soldiers carved in marble to celebrate victory and strength, Lin's design, an ambitious concept of abstract art with no quotes, plaques, or statues, was somber, even morbid, to some. The young designer planted a long wall of black granite in the ground—a wound in the earth expressing the thousands of lives lost in this war.

Despite many challenges, including the inexperienced Lin standing up for her vision in front of the U.S. Congress, her design opened to the public with universal fanfare and tears of gratitude. Twenty-six years later, The American Institute of Architects placed Lin's design on their list of "America's Favorite Architecture."

The journey from concept drawing to the completed project was not without absurdities and compromise. Ross Perot insulted her as an "egg roll" for being Chinese, and Congress defensively placed thematic bronze statues near Lin's project.

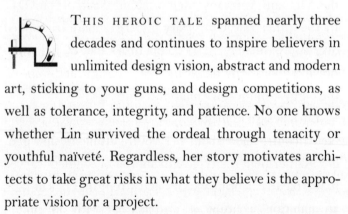 THIS HEROIC TALE spanned nearly three decades and continues to inspire believers in unlimited design vision, abstract and modern art, sticking to your guns, and design competitions, as well as tolerance, integrity, and patience. No one knows whether Lin survived the ordeal through tenacity or youthful naïveté. Regardless, her story motivates architects to take great risks in what they believe is the appropriate vision for a project.

With my proposal for the Hermosa Beach waterfront and pier, I considered the design competition venue a world stage for gutsy thinking by rising stars, innovation from senior architect companies, and all the possibilities in between. I continue to invest time and money to submit proposals to these competitions, despite the odds, because I maintain the passion evidenced in that first design.

The insanity of architects perpetuates the process. With impossible odds, why would one spend the resources on a proposal for New York's 9/11 memorial design competition when the odds are 5,000 to 1 with entries from 6 continents and 63 nations? Wouldn't it be easier to simply sit down with a client and efficiently, methodically design their project rather than confront the statistical madness for success when blindly submitting full-blown architectural presentations to a design jury with which one has no communication or contact at all?

Nonetheless, I continue my entries into such competitions, and I welcome the challenge to design memorials, to support the act of remembrance, to validate the human spirit.

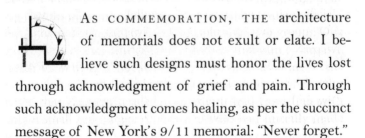 As COMMEMORATION, THE architecture of memorials does not exult or elate. I believe such designs must honor the lives lost through acknowledgment of grief and pain. Through such acknowledgment comes healing, as per the succinct message of New York's 9/11 memorial: "Never forget."

My architecture for spirituality and remembrance informs its visitors. It influences and guides. Such architecture can enliven the human spirit, or it can be a solemn confrontation of the spirit. Though many of my memorial projects are not built, I appreciate designing for memory because the architectural solutions require conviction and devotion. This is a worthwhile calling.

I discuss some of my explorations below. Each resulted in different ideas about honor and remembrance as well as an evolving personal design philosophy.

New England Holocaust Memorial
Boston, Massachusetts

The title on my presentation boards read, "A Canopy over Six Slabs of Earth."

Situated in downtown, my concept offered not a memorial fountain or sculpture but a public space for the remembrance of Holocaust victims.

The design gathered people and their memories under one architectural shelter, an enormous canopy three blocks long. The slightly bent canopy of perforated steel plates folded up and down. Appearing uneven, the roofline depicted tension and uneasiness while serving as a visual landmark for a city with numerous historical landmarks.

At street level, benches were fixed in a scattered pattern surrounded by six huge slabs of stone, each ten by fifty feet, that represented the six million lives lost. Like abstracted tombstones, the slabs rose slightly out of the ground to greet visitors with an implied sense of enclosure and separation from the surrounding traffic. My architecture was to be engaged individually and intimately as well as publicly and as a society.

AIDS Memorial Victims
Key West, Florida

I sought to etch memory in patinated metal plates. This memorial design, done in collaboration with Greg Lombardi, was intentionally not an object like a flag, not a wall like the Vietnam Memorial, and not a sculpture of bronze soldiers.

As with my Holocaust Memorial design, we sought to create a *place.*

In this place made of giant steel plates and vine growth, the crisis known by the simple acronym AIDS enveloped visitors. The sloped metal surfaces, on which victims' names were etched, became the surface on which the visitor also stood as the vertical steel plates continued toward the plaza floor.

Reading the names of lost friends and family, as if inscribed on tombstones, created a powerful and haunting memorial, a place not to be ignored, as the gay community once was.

With the names engraved by two-year periods on heavily textured metal plates, the visitor faced the increasing number of victims from the beginning of the epidemic to the present, from a few names on the first plate to thousands on the second and third plates. Blank steel plates await the names of victims diagnosed HIV positive. The blank plates demand that humanity work harder lest they also be filled.

THE MARTIN LUTHER KING JR. MEMORIAL
Washington, D.C.

In wanting to have the visitor inhabit the memory of Martin Luther King Jr., I created three large cylindrical outdoor rooms to represent King's legacy. The three themes I chose: the Man, the Movement, and the Message.

The journey began on a path paved with gravel to slow the visitor to a meditative pace. Illuminated glass pavers made up the path, giving a sense of lightness and challenging one's complacency. Within each circular room, King's words were etched onto the enveloping interior surface. Without a roof to the rooms, the open sky offered grandeur and awe to the intimacy of the experience.

The first room—made by walls of poured-in-place concrete—stood for the Man as a force and foundation. The material represented the solidity of King's character and courage. The second room, the Movement, expressed power through walls clad in polished stainless-steel panels to symbolize the inherent strength and lasting radiance of King's words. The Message, the third room, was a beacon, a room wrapped by large, cast-glass panels, signifying luminosity and future.

HOLOCAUST AND HUMAN RIGHTS CENTER
University of Maine, Augusta

My design sought to reach toward the future while reflecting on the past. Daringly and dramatically, the east side of my proposed building cantilevered off a hillside. The 6,000-square-foot structure floated toward the future, the horizon, and the views as well as toward a responsible and mindful future. This composition of poise and balance expressed a future of tolerance, progress, and evolution.

Celebrating the diversity of people, the glass exterior of the building was made up of multicolored windows. The richness of colors expressed both the uniqueness of the individual and the beauty of the collective. The pattern of leaning windows accentuated the cantilever, supporting the concept that this project reached for a positive and conscientious future.

9/11 MEMORIAL
Manhattan Beach, California

In calling the design vision "Amphitheater of Remembrance," I composed an area where a community could gather for collective reflection. This proposed project stands for the strength of will that we have developed through sacrifice.

My architecture featured two steel beams recovered from the fallen World Trade Center. The two beams stood upright in representation of the Twin Towers plus the heroism and strength of the human spirit.

I configured amphitheater seating around one side of the steel beams and steps that descended into a reflecting pool on the other. Together, this formed the Amphitheater of Remembrance.

Accessible to the public for gathering and contemplation, the stepped seating gathered around the two twisted, rusted beams as if spectators honoring legendary performers. The inaccessible steps into the water suggested seating for those lost.

CONTRABAND AND FREEDMEN'S CEMETERY MEMORIAL,
Alexandria, Virginia

For the cemetery and memorial park recognizing freed slaves in Virginia, Poon Design created the theme "The Path and the Park."

Our concept was designed around two ideas: to celebrate the historical and spiritual significance of the burial site and to make the land a public gift to the community.

"The Path" began on the east side and followed the ancient cart path that ran through the existing gravesite. Our path was intended to be built of wood and steel memorializing the wood coffins and grave markers that have long since disappeared.

The wood offered warmth and craft to the experience as the Path made a respectful journey through the known excavated portions of the site. Secondary gravel trails branched off the central walk passing between graves and arrived at areas of quiet contemplation.

As the path progressed farther west, it sloped up to reveal the magnitude of the surrounding cemetery. The visitors became aware of the spiritual symbolism of their bodies being lifted as they crossed over and through the memorial. We intended the graves to be marked with split slabs of alabaster, a luminous white stone.

In "the Park," as the visitors took the rising trek to the west side of our memorial, they passed through a grove of maple trees. The ground rose in the form of a large grass mound: the center of a new community park. In this public space, visitors discovered a wall of alabaster blocks inscribed with the names of those buried, one name per block to allow for future inscriptions as geologic explorations continued.

 WHETHER PROFOUND OR merely descriptive, my goal is primarily *communication*. Architecture, whether for a memorial, a home, an office building, or a temple, should communicate a message. Architecture offers a physical expression of remembrance, security, stability, or faith; in essence the heart of a design.

In addition, during the process of designing, from the first sketch on a piece of scrap paper to the final polish of a granite floor at the construction site, the architect's design must convince the invested parties that these somewhat arbitrary artistic ideas are indeed appropriate for their project.

In her early twenties, Maya Lin did this before a daunting audience, the entire country of the United States. For me, I communicate day-to-day designs to my team, my engineers, contractors, city agencies, and, most importantly of all, my clients.

The design itself, whether a memorial or a school is (1) a communication of ideas, which then requires (2) the design articulated in pencil drawings, computer renderings, and wood and acrylic models as well as through e-mails, telephone calls, face-to-face meetings, and public presentations.

Despite having the talents of a designer, the most sought-after and creative soul has no chance of succeeding as an architect if he or she doesn't comprehend the importance of communication. Wouldn't you say all who walk the earth would benefit from such an understanding?

part two

ARCHITECTURE FROM THE OUTSIDE

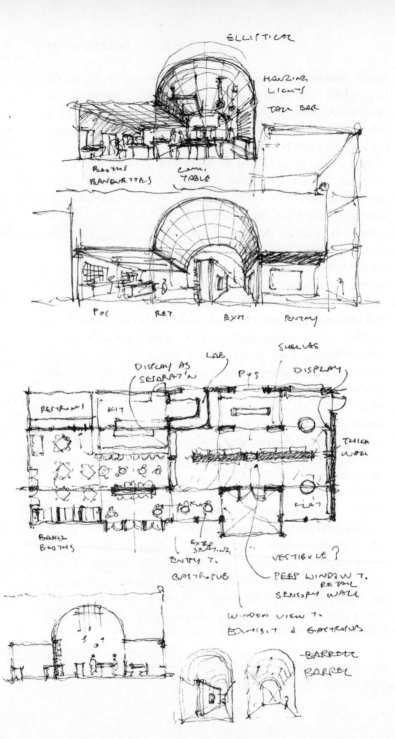

ELLIPTICAL

HANGING
LIGHTS

TALL BAR

BOOTHS
BANQUETTES

COMM.
TABLE

POC   RET.   EXH.   ENTRY

SHELVES

DISPLAY AS
SEPARATION

LAB   POS   DISPLAY

RESTROOMS   KIT

THICK
WALL

FLAT

BANK
BOOTHS

EXTR.
SEATING

ENTRY T.
GASTROPUB

VESTIBULE?

PEEP WINDOW T.
RETAIL
SENSORY WALL

WINDOW VIEW T.
EXHIBIT & GASTROPUB

BARREL
BARREL

CANDYLAND

Come with me and you'll be in a
world of pure imagination.
We'll begin with a spin traveling in the
world of my creation.
There is no life I know to compare with
pure imagination.

ROALD DAHL

WHETHER GENE WILDER'S 1971 *Willy Wonka & the Chocolate Factory* or Johnny Depp's 2005 *Charlie and the Chocolate Factory*, the essence of each film embraces candy and architecture.

Yes, it is a story about Charlie, a fortunate boy, and Willy, an inventive designer—and their hopes and ambitions. This story is also about the creation of another world, the design of a visionary existence. In both films, and the original Roald Dahl book, who could forget the architecture of theatrical imagery, fantastical scale, vivid colors, rich textures, vibrant lights, and pulsing rhythms? Such things are the fabric of architecture, and, of course, the Great Glass Elevator.

CAN CANDY BE the soul of architectural projects? Poon Design explored this notion for two retail clients: Chicago-based Vosges Haut-Chocolat and Beverly Hills–based Sugarfina. For the founders of these two companies, candy was a religion. Though Poon Design's projects were under the guise of consumer retail design, we believed the results of our work possessed the gravitas of sacred architecture. We harnessed the architectural power of storytelling as one might preach a particular message.

For Vosges, we first completed their West Coast flagship store, then followed up with an ambitious design for a chocolate factory and national headquarters on the bank of the Chicago River. Founder and chocolatier Katrina Markoff referred to this grand facility as a "chocolate lifestyle house."

MY REFERENCE TO religion is not so much about deities as about a grounding system of belief. Katrina, client and a soulful artist, believes in the healing and enlightening powers of chocolate. As such, Vosges upheld a dutiful search for authenticity and truth, whether in the ingredients of their gourmet confections, in architectural ideas and solutions, or in global initiatives serving the environment. You will see what I mean regarding architecture and truth.

For our design of Vosges's retail store in Beverly Hills, 110 feet long and only 14 feet wide, we divided the store into three zones. We created a procession of three transformative, chocolate-focused experiences:

PEOPLE

PRODUCT

PROCESS

The three experiences were also thought of this way:

ENTRY

ENGAGEMENT

EXPLANATION

Lastly, using a second architecturally driven title, we studied *The Wonderful Wizard of Oz* and conceived our sequence as:

YELLOW BRICK ROAD

EMERALD CITY

BEHIND THE CURTAIN

The first experience, the entry, served the arrival as well as the gathering of people. This zone featured an intimate café setting with an eclectic mix of lounge furniture. To the right of the front door, a sensory installation of woods, spices, and herbs depicted the story of chocolate around the world.

The second experience, the marketplace, captured the soaring spirit of merchandising and sales. An intricately hand-painted, double-vaulted ceiling capped the narrow room. A church-like groin vault provided a dramatic architectural backdrop and also referenced Gothic cathedrals.

We called the third experience the "Chocolate Theater." Here, audience members witnessed chocolatiers concocting tasty treats such as the creative combination of chocolate, fruitwood-smoked uncured bacon, and alderwood salt. This room presented process and creation, with "creation" used intentionally.

The big unifying design idea was Moroccan plaster arch gateways between each of the three areas. For these arches, I wanted to get from the drawing phase to reality as simply as possible. I proposed local talent to execute the Moroccan arches. The other option, working with plaster craftsmen and guilds in the country of Morocco, would then be unnecessary and frankly kind of nuts.

I suggested to the client, "There are number of excellent plaster workers in Southern California who could make your Moroccan-style archways. No problem. In fact, this is Hollywood," I continued with my pitch, "and many of the builders who create movie sets are the best artisans around."

The client found no satisfaction in my statements. My idea was not a solution, not an option. She declared, "I want Moroccan arches, not Moroccan-style arches. And I mean from the country of Morocco." She sought arches fully articulated with historically accurate Moorish details, carved by Moorish hands.

Custom-fabricating extremely delicate arches to fit into a preexisting Beverly Hills retail space was enough of a challenge, but the real question that concerned me was why spend the energy, money, and time to work with plaster artists six thousand miles away? How would we coordinate the packing and shipping, pass through airports and customs, uncrate in Los Angeles, install at the site piece by giant, delicate piece, plus stay within Vosges's moderate budget and accelerated schedule? Why should we do this when the local stucco and cement plaster shop a mere twenty minutes away could make arches nearly identical to the client's vision?

The client's position was exact and unforgiving. There was no room for negotiation. Though Los Angeles–produced arches might be identical in shape to arches from Marrakesh, the Los Angeles product could never replicate Moroccan *soul*.

Moroccan arches come from Morocco, not from Hollywood.

As I said, truth and authenticity.

In support of the client's devotion to the genuine,

Poon Design did indeed work with plaster artists from Marrakesh who used the ancient tools standard to the artisanal hand-casting process. Though the shipping and installation of the arches were no easy task, collaborating with the artists in Morocco did indeed keep things in budget, since labor and materials were economical.

The result: arches that could accurately and deeply be called Moroccan. All visitors stop and stare in awe at the craftsmanship.

AFTER THE OPENING of this boutique, Vosges commissioned Poon Design to design the "chocolate lifestyle house." This was no mere residence.

To date, the first phase of construction has been completed: the full-blown, 43,000-square-foot chocolate factory, accompanied by Vosges's corporate headquarters. When the second phase of the project is fully realized, the complex will also offer a chocolate museum, retail store, gastropub, event spaces, and a community park with a dock to the Chicago River.

This project supported the company's mission that chocolate sustains the substance of our existence. The culture of Vosges was not a religion per se, but the owner/creator had faith in chocolate. Her company's emblem depicts *their* circle of life: "Falling in love leads to inspiration, leads to action, leads to experience," which leads you back to falling in love.

The candy treats were not merely for eating and retail sales. The chocolate concoctions fed our well-being and our spirits. Our client often signed her memos with "Peace, love and chocolate—Katrina."

Aside from engaging one's taste buds, this visitor center involved the eyes, ears, and nose, with sensory exhibits of aromas and textures of each culinary ingredient. Large murals of various countries indicated both the source of the ingredients and Vosges's cultural inspirations. Such precedent inspired our architectural details. Our process was driven by an eclecticism of decorative flourishes.

The Buenos Aires ironwork on the exterior of the building cast intricate shadows on the brick facades. The street-facing facade, 175 feet long, was painted royal purple top to bottom, the company's trade dress color. Period newspaper clippings from around the globe covered the walls of the atrium, floor to ceiling, wall to wall. Hand-painted Viennese tile work, industrial steel and glass doors and walls, black ceiling tiles with high floral relief, Parisian Art Nouveau prints, Suzani fabrics from India, and a Victorian garden maze—these architectural features and hundreds more delivered an experience that blanketed the visitor in a tapestry of cultures, people, and beliefs.

As we "traveled" around the world to satisfy our design imagination, we confronted our own country's Department of Homeland Security. This chocolate factory, being such a large food production facility, could be, however unintentionally, a site ripe for terrorism.

According to Homeland Security, terrorists could transform food widely distributed around America into biological weapons. To prevent the corruption by lethal chemicals of international shipments of Vosges chocolates, our architecture had to incorporate national security protocol. For example, we designed high partitions for the candy tour so that a terrorist posing as a customer could not throw dangerous chemicals into batches of chocolate under production.

The architecture of candy isn't all fun and sweet.

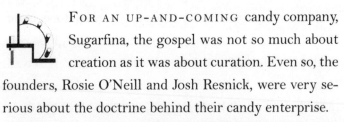 FOR AN UP-AND-COMING candy company, Sugarfina, the gospel was not so much about creation as it was about curation. Even so, the founders, Rosie O'Neill and Josh Resnick, were very serious about the doctrine behind their candy enterprise.

Was our design for Sugarfina to be just another candy store, or would it instead become a temple dedicated to hundreds of gourmet sweets? Were the founders mere business owners, or were they curators of a museum that catered to the connoisseur?

The world certainly seemed full of candy stores, from the old-school See's Candies to your standard convenience store to ambitious commercial ventures with clever monikers like Dylan's Candy Bar, or kosher stores like Munchies.

Sugarfina's approach was like no other. Interestingly, the founders brainstormed their concept on a third date while watching none other than the film *Willy Wonka*.

Sugarfina's thesis was this: If an adult of discerning tastes enjoyed gourmet treats such as rare wine, smoked cheese, foie gras pâté, omakase sushi, and aged steaks, where could this individual find candy at the same level of epicurean enjoyment and decadence?

Sugarfina was no main-street Americana confectionary, such as those that sell lollipops made of glucose and food coloring. In stark contrast, imagine, if you will, a Sugarfina "bento box" of champagne-infused gummy bears from the Bavarian region of Germany, chocolates with kumquats, cherries, and strawberries from the Greek Isles, bacon-and-white-chocolate pretzel bites, and pumpkin-pie caramels.

Similar to the outreach integral to Vosges Haut-Chocolat, Rosie and Josh of Sugarfina considered themselves diplomats bridging their diverse world of sugary treats and our pedestrian taste buds. They traveled the world, meeting with local artisans as well as national dignitaries, to broaden their own palates.

Sugarfina was their dream company replete with dream job descriptions.

In subscribing to this fantasy-come-true, Poon Design imagined a dream-like environment with walls constructed of sweets. With the sensation of relaxing in the clouds, you would believe you had arrived in candy heaven.

We concocted a design narrative to guide the development of our ideas: a fairy-tale of an apothecary drawn from Lewis Carroll's *Alice's Adventures in Wonderland*.

Our design was white. I mean the white white of things such as clouds, such as cotton, such as a dream, such as heaven with only accents splashed here and there with the company's trademark sky blue. Like both a gallery and a laboratory, hundreds, maybe thousands, of tiny, clear cubes about two inches square appeared to float off the wall, as they were delicately arranged on thin white steel shelves.

We then filled the store with little drawers. Hundreds of drawers everywhere. Though our cabinet designs had standard doors, we designed the doors to appear as if there were an endless sea of drawer fronts and knobs.

We delivered an architectural mystery, a question of what lies beyond. What is inside all those little drawers? What secrets, gifts, treats, recipes, and surprises lie out of reach?

A "Candy Concierge," like a hotel caretaker, treated

Sugarfina visitors to a customized shopping experience, as any sommelier, tailor, or barista would share deep knowledge of his or her artisanal trade.

SACRED ARCHITECTURE, ASIDE from seeking truths, offers allegories, myths, impressions, and a shape to faith—all in three architectural projects for candy: the Vosges flagship store, the Vosges chocolate factory and the iconic Sugarfina.

IMPLIED SYMMETRY

SYMMETRY "W/ A TWIST"

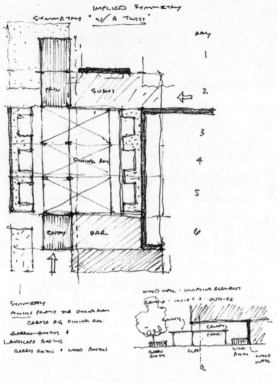

BAY

1

2

3

4

5

6

PAN   SUSHI

DINING RM

CANPY   BAR

SYMMETRY
POSSIBLE FRAME THE DINING ROOM
CREATE BIG DINING RM.
GARDEN BOOTHS &
LANDSCAPE BOOTHS
GARDEN BOOTHS & WOOD BOOTHS

WOOD WALL : UNIFYING ELEMENT
CANOPY : INSIDE + OUTSIDE

CANOPY
CANOPY
CANOPY/STONE
GARDEN
BOOTH   GLAZ   WOOD
BOOTH   WOOD
WALL

KABUKI
BACK DROP

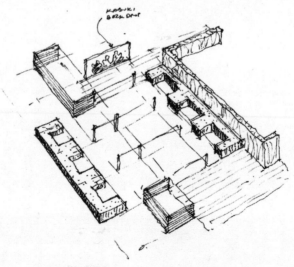

I WANT TO DESIGN
EVERYTHING

If architects weren't arrogant, they wouldn't be architects. I don't know a modest good architect.

PHILIP JOHNSON

FROM GRADUATE SCHOOL, I took a summer break to design a friend's restaurant, and that was when I realized just how much I wanted to design everything.

I needed relief from the long, damp, and gray winters of Cambridge, where the snow begins its winter fall on Thanksgiving and the sun hides for months after. A New England spring is sublime but slow in blooming. The chance to go to sunny Los Angeles for a project would, I thought, be the perfect mental and physical break before my fourth and final year at the Harvard Graduate School of Design. Twenty years on, LA is still my home.

My good friend since high school was an MBA student at UCLA. She and her classmate and boyfriend (they are now married) authored a business plan—to launch a café—as an assignment for their entrepreneurial class. They had to create the concept, analyze the finances, find the funding, open the café, own and operate it as a thriving business, and form an exit plan to sell it for a profit. This may not seem like such a big deal in these days of coffee shops on every corner, but back in 1991, it was a fresh concept.

This business plan was so convincing to my friends' professor that he offered seed money to put it into action. Their united marketing acumen and my modest but tangible architecture bona fides combined to create the feeling that this could really work.

I'm a great planner but somehow forgot that I needed a place to stay for this Los Angeles summer. Luckily— very luckily, as you'll see—my old friend introduced me to her friend Martha, who was leaving her apartment empty for the summer. Martha lived in Westwood near the UCLA campus and was temporarily moving to the San Francisco area to work with her mother. I married Martha seven years later.

To make ends meet and add to my résumé while the café plans took form, I found a summer job with Angelil/ Graham, a small, talented architecture office on trendy Melrose Avenue—a colorful street of tourist shops, designer boutiques, secondhand clothing stores, tattoo parlors, and diverse restaurants.

I was just a staff designer, but I loved being a staff

designer in LA during the day. At all other times that summer, it was all café designing.

WHENEVER WE COULD find slivers of time together, the two MBA students and I worked obsessively to make the café a reality. Early mornings, late nights, and weekends, we brainstormed on everything from layout to drink names to store hours. I hand-drafted (not many computers back then) sheets and sheets of designs so we could get a permit for construction when the time came. I made a large-scale model out of white foamcore, the go-to, easy-to-cut sheets favored by architects for rough model making. (This model, my first professional model as part of a real commission, burned in a house fire along with many of the original drawings for the café, which quickly taught me that although architecture is both a process and product, it is the end product that has the most impact—a restaurant, a house, a city hall. It is the building, rarely the model, that is central to creating a name and career—though some well-known architects have indeed achieved initial great fame from their groundbreaking visions represented in a mere model or two.)

TwoPart—the name of our café—was based on the existing space we inherited in the building. We took advantage of two distinct entrances—one from the street and one from the parking lot in the back—by placing the counter and kitchen in the middle; voilà, two parts. Each room had its own character. One was an informal room with lounge furniture and even a sofa, which was, believe it or not, an unusual sight for the time in any retail space that wasn't selling sofas; the other was more active and bustling, with high stools and tables and brighter lights.

The coffee chains weren't ubiquitous yet (Starbuck's was fairly new and just had its first seventy locations nationwide; currently it has twenty-five thousand and counting), and what we think of as the bohemian cafés of the Beat poets, from Bleecker Street in New York to North Beach in San Francisco, were still few and far between. The three famous coffeehouses in LA at that time were Lulu's Alibi, Insomnia, and Cacao—all three having in common a blend of independently branded coffee, a somewhat European atmosphere, cheesecake and basic pastries, and a culture driven by local art, poetry readings, and live music performances.

Besides our floor plan and interior design, TwoPart added something else to the coffeehouse formula: We offered world-class desserts from an acclaimed local chef who prepared pastries at the restaurants of Wolfgang Puck.

The strategy was simple. If, after a movie or casual

dinner with friends, you wanted to have a dessert that rivaled offerings at places helmed by Puck and Jeremiah Towers, TwoPart was a tantalizing option. No hassle, no reservation, easy parking, and a great atmosphere. If you were out with friends on a budget but looking for a great dessert to go with great coffee, and you wanted something different and better than day-old cheesecake, TwoPart would be the answer.

 FOR ME, TWOPART was the testing ground for an idea that to this day my company is still exploring and reimplementing: the idea that an architect or an architecture studio can offer a package of cohesive design ideas. Comprehensive, integrated design services. Yes, at that time many architecture companies offered the triple-threat services of architecture, interior design, and graphics, but I wanted to take it several notches higher and rungs deeper.

For TwoPart, in collaboration with the two owners, I drove everything that required a creative and aesthetic agenda: the storefront design; the interior and lighting; the furniture that I selected and we refurbished with our own hands; the custom-designed furniture that I made on my apartment balcony; the marketing and advertising strategies; the graphic design of all collateral materials and products that included the logo, from T-shirts to matchbooks, from menus to cups.

I selected the music that would transition throughout the day to suit myriad energy levels, from up-and-about early birds to a buzzing daytime crowd, then to a sophisticated evening audience, then winding down with an after-hours repertoire—all before the word "playlist" became part of our daily lexicon.

I interviewed and chose the artists whose work would be featured on our walls each month. Once we opened, I would curate the shows, lay out the sequence on the walls, even design the invitations. I provided direction on employees' wardrobe and uniform. I selected all the china and flatware. Ultimately, so I could say I walked the walk and espressoed the espresso, I worked the machines for our customers to explore the art of making the perfect cappuccino, which later became an ongoing competition among the TwoPart baristas.

All the aspects of the café, from music to the exquisitely prepared cap in a tall glass, were in my mind part of the architecture in the sense that architecture is a cohesive, integrated, comprehensive experience and brand.

Creating a single source of design services had both creative benefits and business advantages. Besides one-stop shopping and a single contract, a client would only need to explain his or her grand vision once: inspirations, stories, and expectations. The client could make a connection with one creative team and expect to have a coherent project in the end.

TWO PART WENT INTO construction in the fall of 1991 as I headed back east to school. I had the satisfaction of completing my time at Harvard with the knowledge that my first commission, though small, was already under construction. And when our café opened in January 1992, I had the overwhelming feeling that many architects experience with the completion of each project: the intimidating and humbling understanding that architecture is created not in the abstract of pen and paper but in the reality of brick and mortar and that architecture is created for use, not display.

One wonderful evening, one of the owners picked me up at LAX, and we drove directly to TwoPart for opening night. The parking lot was full, and as we entered, the place was abuzz. We beamed like proud parents.

People in lively conversation in the chairs I had designed and constructed; couples lounging hand in hand on the sofa I had chosen the slipcover for; employees buzzing around the kitchen; smiles as customers discovered the other room around the diagonal wall; small crowds gathering next to the hundred-foot-long copper painted wall, which over time would develop a beautiful patina of handprints; an individual emerging from the Blue Bathroom, so named because the walls and ceiling were painted an electric blue; a nervous man trying to get the home phone number (no cell phones or e-mail addresses back then) of an attractive woman, the two of them standing at a countertop made of simple plywood but laminated with aluminum sheets with a pattern of raised dots; the music of the Indigo Girls quietly filling the room through speakers I had chosen and wired, music that I had picked for this first evening of customers. And on the front facade and the back door, a big red "2" in Palatino font, the simple but effective logo I had created for this entire endeavor.

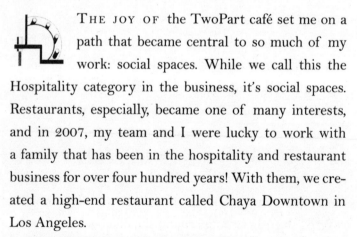 THE JOY OF the TwoPart café set me on a path that became central to so much of my work: social spaces. While we call this the Hospitality category in the business, it's social spaces. Restaurants, especially, became one of many interests, and in 2007, my team and I were lucky to work with a family that has been in the hospitality and restaurant business for over four hundred years! With them, we created a high-end restaurant called Chaya Downtown in Los Angeles.

The studio team of Poon Design led by Principal John Kim and Project Manager Bryan Bethem designed every aspect of this 210-seat modern Japanese/French fusion restaurant.

Along with our restaurant interior designer Robert Weimer, graphic designers Sue and Danny Yee, and landscape designer Elizabeth Low, we designed the architecture, interior design, lighting, landscape, furniture, interior decor, menu, website, all graphic products from business cards to matchbooks to special event packages, and advertising.

We also selected and hung works of art by artists such as Ajioka from Tokyo and the famed Stuart Haygarth from London, assisted in music selection, and provided commentary on uniform design—to list a few unexpected disciplines. We won an international design award for our work and helped create a dynamic, profitable business and social space for our client.

 I AM INTERESTED in designing *everything*. This interest was put into action over two decades ago and continues with my company today.

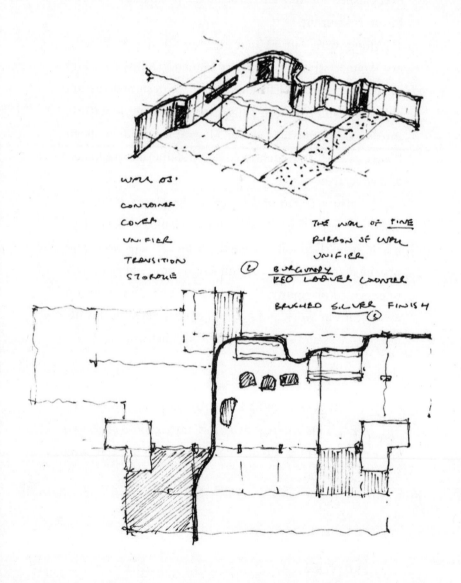

WALL AS:

CONTAINER

COVER

UNIFIER

TRANSITION

STORAGE

THE WALL OF TIME

RIBBON OF WALL

UNIFIER

② BURGUNDY
RED LACQUER COUNTER

BRUSHED SILVER FINISH
③

TO SEE AND BE SEEN:

ARCHITECTURE FOR FASHION

*Architecture stimulates fashion. It's like hunger and
thirst; you need them both.*

KARL LAGERFELD

A CLOTHING STORE should do more than merely
stock, display, and sell. The architecture of such a store
should do more than be a big container with shelves and
hooks.

Colleague Brooke Hodge wrote in her book and associated exhibit, *Skin + Bones: Parallel Practices in Fashion
and Architecture,* "Both architecture and fashion are based
on the human body and on ideas of space, volume, and
movement. Each functions as shelter or wrapping for
the body—a mediating layer between the body and the
environment—and can express personal, political, and
cultural identity."

In her 2007 exhibit at Los Angeles' Museum of Contemporary Art, the comparison continues, even extending toward techniques of construction and fabrication: folding, wrapping, draping, forming, coloring, and so on.

TWENTY-FIVE YEARS AGO, when I was with the Santa Monica architecture studio KAA, Nicole Miller, a high-fashion clothing designer, commissioned us to design a retail store in Boca Raton, Florida. Nicole Miller's creations were vividly colored and patterned, drawing inspiration from contemporary art and architecture. Not only was this high-profile client ideal for us as young architects, but so too was her project. She sought a novel architectural statement for this flagship store that in turn would be compelling enough to brand all her future locations throughout the United States.

Before I get into the specific design ideas that parallel the fashion world and architecture, let's briefly examine the architecture industry's typical idea of creating a physical brand for a retail space. The solution for most architects and their corporate clients, whether clothing, computers, or coffee, is to simply generate a palette of materials and fixtures, then replicate it in every upcoming store. This approach of a consistent palette offers an easy solution for a physical brand, also known as "trade dress."

With this obvious but only somewhat effective method, a flagship store might have, for example, a palette of dark oak floors, taupe-painted walls, gray-stained cabinets, brass detailing, an accent stripe of hunter green, and a few interesting Italian light fixtures. This is the palette. This is the brand. This is the trade dress.

For each future location, whether Las Vegas, Boise, or Shanghai, the same—exactly the same—elements are installed. Offering an easily recognizable assembly of colors and materials to the consumer, this tactic establishes a company's physical brand while causing little brain damage when a company expands and builds in new cities. In addition, meeting a known construction budget, sourcing common materials, using the same vendors, and building standardized fabrication details also offer efficiency. Heck, you might not even need to pay an architect much if you are building the same design over and over again.

Whether the store is big or small, whether the owner spends $500,000 or $50 million, whether the store is on a beach or in the woods, consistency proves to be successful.

Great, right?

Does the term "cookie cutter" come to mind?

 WITH THE FLAGSHIP project for Nicole Miller, I questioned why the architectural brand for nearly all companies is created by merely replicating materials and color. I proposed a new idea: The architectural brand should be created by offering consistency in architectural *experience*.

Allow me to expound. There is no doubt that the type of wood flooring and light fixtures are part of a customer's experience, but I suggested to the Nicole Miller team that how one experiences a store can be based on richer ideas like spatial configuration and sequence, proportions and scale, or sound and structure.

Although a palette of common materials might address what you see, and even what you touch, it does not address what the entire body feels as it moves through a space. Imagine, if you will, how an experience changes when the floor level and associated sightline are altered by a few steps, or as one transitions from a dramatic, grand space immediately to an intimate niche. Such is the power of architecture beyond the color of an accent paint.

Certainly one could argue that how a visitor engages the total experience of a store through all the senses, including the beats of background music and how the feet sound when moving from a tile floor to carpet, may still be considered cookie-cutter when replicated over and over again. I counter that the deeper and more detailed the experience operates on one's consciousness and even subconsciousness, the less it is a cookie cutter.

Without thinking about the richer impressions that

architecture can make, you merely get that repetitive Pinkberry or Starbuck's, looking exactly the same, offering no subtlety in sensations and experience.

So on to the design for our groundbreaking Nicole Miller store. My premise about fashion and architecture speaks mostly about the physical similarities, such as color, textures, and shapes. For my Nicole Miller design (done in collaboration with Greg Lombardi), I chose to explore the fashion world, not as a physical thing but as an *event*.

The world of fashion is not only about fabrics, cuts, necklines, and silhouettes, which are all physical items. I saw the fashion world as theater. As an event, I saw it as a dramatic experience, scenes to be played out.

With this philosophical framework, I interpreted the Nicole Miller shoppers not merely as customers but as models on the iconic fashion runway. My thinking resulted in several innovative store features, but the main concept was in shaping the floor. In most retail stores, the floor is usually nothing more than flat and level. My floor design started normal at the entry, but several steps into the shop, the floor ramped up a few feet, gracefully rising toward the back, circled around, and finally descended back to terra firma, facing the entry door.

Along this theatrical path, this imaginary catwalk

from my mind, clothes were displayed with dramatic lighting of various tones of warmth, accents, and intensity.

The main floor of this design was concrete, but the elevated floor in hardwood provided a subtle change of sound and feel as one entered my make-believe world of supermodels. Circulating along the store's short journey, you could see and be seen, as is the common motto in the world of style and celebrity.

Executed well, the constructed project was not a theme-park Parisian fashion show. My metaphor of the runway was an inspiration and an abstract concept. The theme was implicit, not in your face.

For those such as a design critic seeking a story, we had a full-blown theory about fashion and architecture as well as a critique of standard boring flagship and roll-out stores. For those who were unaware of our design narrative, the store was just a welcoming space that offered interesting areas that felt different but enjoyable.

Our spatial ideas were intended to be consistent, but the development could take on variations. In not specifying the exact same black granite tiles over and over again for each location, my prototype of a sculptural experience in space and time allowed new Nicole Miller locations to have varying identities that suited the communities they served. A downtown location selling to professionals in suits should be different than a location on the pier selling to beach families in board shorts.

Hypothetically, for a small location in a tiny shopping district, perhaps the ramped floor is made of casual-looking plywood panels. For a San Francisco Union Square location, maybe the ramped catwalk is made of distinguished polished marble. For a funky industrial area in an up-and-coming neighborhood, the catwalk could be made to feel industrial in colored concrete.

Whether the materials were similar from store to store or slightly adapted to a location, budget, and expectations, the brand was something a customer *felt* as consistent. The success of my architecture here was in its power to imply and suggest, not treat a visitor like a hungry child seeking the red and yellow of McDonald's.

RECENTLY, THESE IDEAS were tested. Enzoani, a wedding-gown brand sold at locations around the globe, retained Poon Design for an exercise similar to that of Nicole Miller. Enzoani was expanding and sought an inventive flagship that would set the architectural voice for bridal stores launching in many countries.

Taking the same approach, but with design maturity, experience in construction, and advancements with digital fabrication, we employed a powerful philosophy that surpassed the still-done-today approach of stores using two colors of paint and a feature wall of stone. (Or something like that.)

Our flagship for Enzoani was constructed in Riyadh, Saudi Arabia, where I traveled and had the joy of being stuck in a customs line for over eight hours. Eight hours. Standing. No water. No food. No bathroom breaks. No sitting on the floor to use a computer or read a book.

Our design for this client studied two aspects of the wedding ceremony: the mysterious and alluring wedding veil and the facets of the diamond ring. These two themes influenced our striking design of large folded metal plates, powder coated in bright white (the diamond facets). We then perforated the plates with tiny holes in a pattern that, in an allusion to draping silk, at times obscured the view through and at other times revealed the view in its entirety (the veil).

These eight-foot-tall bent metal plates created dressing rooms, display zones, family gathering areas, and backdrops for merchandising. The veil quality offered complete privacy for changing but openness for merchandise to be featured. We designed the architecture so that elements of a number of stores could be fabricated in a single factory, shipped flat to international cities, and assembled in place.

LIKE NICOLE MILLER, the Enzoani architecture was both obvious and not at all so. No one experienced our Riyadh design and said, "Oh, hey, this looks like a big veil and a giant diamond." In fact, this never happened. The refinement of the idea was intentionally developed as understated.

As in life, some of the best messages are told through a soft whisper, rather than a bold shout. With elephants dancing in the background.

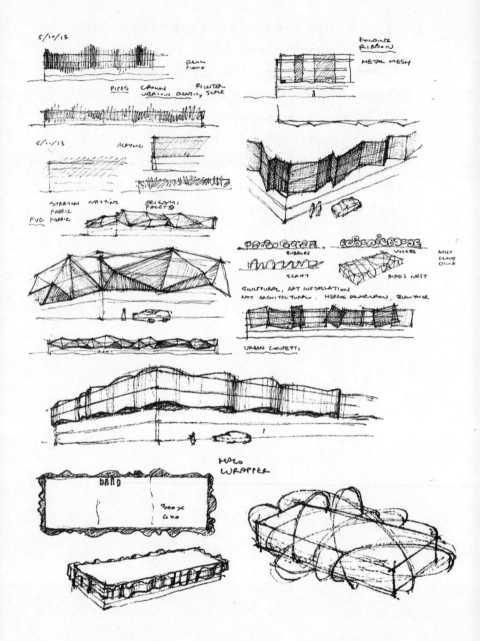

5/10/13

RENZO PIANO

PIPES CROWN RICHTER
VARIOUS DENSITY SCALE

5/11/13 ACRYLIC

STRETCH NETTING ORIGAMI
FABRIC FACETED
PVC FABRIC

FOLDING RIBBON

METAL MESH

BUBBLES VOSGES MIST CLOUD DIKE

SCARF BIRD'S NEST

SCULPTURAL, ART INSTALLATION
NOT ARCHITECTURAL. HERZOG DE MEURON, BJARKE

URBAN CONFETTI

HALO WRAPPER

DAAD

300 x 600

THE CURIOUS THING
ABOUT STYLE

I realize that having a style would be very beneficial for my practice from a marketing standpoint, but I can't do it. Each place has a distinct culture and function, which for me requires an appropriate answer.

CESAR PELLI

I WAS ASKED in a recent interview, "What is your *style?*"

This question is often asked not just of architects but of creative people from all sorts of industries: fashion, graphics, advertising, cuisine, music, film, etc. The media typically aim to capture one's design philosophy in one easily digestible sound bite.

Many interior decorators have a packaged response. I hear words like "eclectic," "warm and welcoming," "contemporary yet timeless." I am not sure what kind of design results from a mash-up of clichés.

Architects have a harder time speaking about their style. New York architect Hugh Hardy, one of my past employers, argued that once you answer the dreaded question, your audience will constantly assess your work against the tag you've given yourself.

What is style, after all?

Though they've completed an extensive education and a 250-page graduate school thesis, many architects simply can't and won't summarize their creative philosophy in twenty words or less. For some, "style" is a bad word. We shouldn't have to sell ourselves with an elevator pitch.

Some well-known architects who will talk about their design style do so with clever labels. Steven Ehrlich, based in Los Angeles, calls his work "Regional Modernism." New Mexico architect Antoine Predock is a self-described "Cosmic Modernist." Herzog & de Meuron of Switzerland have been coined "Elemental Reductivists." From New York, Steven Holl's work involves "typology, phenomenology, and existentialism." Pritzker Prize architects such as Los Angeles' Frank Gehry, New York's Richard Meier, or Japan's Tadao Ando have been accused of formulaic design. Many suggest that all their buildings look the same.

Though arguably true, is this so bad? Don't all the songs by the Beatles or all the piano sonatas by Beethoven sound similar? Don't most Prada shoes, Room & Board sofas, or Manet paintings look the same? All of David Mamet's works read similarly, as do those by Edgar Allan Poe.

Over a lifetime, many artists pursue a personal agenda that one shouldn't, but can easily, dismiss as producing work that is monotonously all the same.

If this repetitive, creative work is enjoyable, possibly great or even genius, is it so bad that all the work is alike? Does anyone complain about Apple products being somewhat identical—oh, that minimal simplicity, the intuitive functions, the beautiful Zen-like philosophy?

Personally, I do think much of Frank Gehry's work looks similar, but I like all of his architectural creations and can't wait to see the next. People probably said the same about Frank Lloyd Wright or Michelangelo.

I see no problem here.

I do find it annoying that the media's analysis of a string of similar-looking projects by one architect assigns arbitrary theories for why each one is vastly different. In being careful to not call an architect's portfolio repetitive, some writers use colorful explanations for the same designs.

For example, one writer might state that Gehry was exploring how a fallen city rises from ashes. "But in *this* project" (one that looks the same as another), Gehry was expressing the blossoming of a flower. "And *here*" (another identical design), Gehry was fascinated with the outward beam of the sun's rays. All this mumbo-jumbo just to avoid saying this performing arts center looks like the architect's designs for the last three.

IT IS MY turn to respond to the universal question about style. I would hope my answer is complex without being pretentious or trite.

At the time of the interview, I answered in two parts: product and process.

My product, meaning the final structure, is driven by *juxtaposition*.

My process is inspired by *jazz*, with its spontaneity and improvisational spirit.

THE JUXTAPOSITION OF THINGS

I enjoy combining things, whether comfortable or awkward, to see what might arise. Sometimes the modern with the traditional, the handcrafted with the machine-made, or brilliant colors with earthy hues, just to name a few. My approach isn't simply an interior decorator's standard eclecticism, like Cape Cod candles paired with ancient Asian tapestries.

Philosophies also can be juxtaposed, such as surrealism with hip-hop plus a dash of the Hellenistic period, or maybe Zen with anime.

I explore juxtaposition not only in superficial theories of colors and textures but also in the way architecture is made. Some of my buildings have been constructed by volunteer hands in the middle of a forest. Some of my buildings are prefabricated by the most sophisticated of software and prototyping machinery. Some of my buildings blend these two construction approaches to deliver an unexpected result.

For a food blogger's residence in Pasadena, Poon Design juxtaposed the technology of parametric algorithms onto polyethylene, the material used to make household kitchen cutting boards, for a large rear-yard canopy.

For a Buddhist meditation retreat in Virginia, we created a balcony guardrail from a galvanized off-the-shelf steel frame entirely wrapped with natural twine made from hemp. Yes, you can smoke it.

For the University of California, Riverside, our student-center design combined traditional redbrick and white limestone exterior finishes with a high, sleek glass curtain wall and oversized zinc shingles to create a monumental, iconic statement.

At our Mendocino Farms restaurants, we blended a funky old-school vibe of chalkboard walls, vaudeville-inspired signage, and clothespins with luxurious Carrara marble, walnut planks, stainless steel trim, and custom furniture.

Juxtaposition typifies not only my artistic approach but also my interests in life. I like Brahms, and I also like *American Idol.* I like the classic techniques of Rembrandt and the easy-on-the-eyes images of Pop Art. I like omakase sushi with a soda as well as McDonald's with sake. I wear Gucci with the Gap, love Nan Goldin and fashion-magazine photography. I read biographies but also comic books. I like watching Ping-Pong and the Super Bowl, reality shows that follow CNN.

I like the diversity and the messiness. I like unexpected results.

Is this my *style*, or simply what drives me?

JAZZ-LIKE

What can architecture learn from jazz? Specifically, what can the process of architecture learn from how musicians create jazz?

Architects are bogged down by details and calculations that ensure a structure won't collapse. We are also burdened by budgets, city codes, and construction limitations. The nature of our daily work is often slow and tedious.

A building can take years or decades—or longer— from start to finish. Even today, projects drag like the three generations required to build Rome's St. Peter's Basilica. One of my residential designs, an admittedly humongous house now in its eleventh year, is finally nearing completion. Whether a clothing shop or a football stadium, the architectural process is sluggish and overwrought. At times painfully so.

With graphic design, on the other hand, a logo can be designed efficiently. In less than a month, boom, the logo appears on a website. (Sorry, my graphic artist friends, I know it is much more complicated than this, but in comparison ...)

In jazz, a group of musicians sit at their instruments, glance at each other, perhaps a wink, then a smile, and boom: music. The jam session begins, and the audience immediately enjoys sound and rhythm. Yes, they bring years of playing, alone and with others, to the club, but still, they are able to be spontaneous and in sync very quickly.

Spontaneity and improvisation are often used to describe jazz. As a classically trained pianist, I was taught a mind-set common in architecture, where at great lengths and with agony, each and every move is careful, conditioned, and rigorously rational. When performing Bach, I wouldn't just toss the sheet music onto the stage floor and riff on a toccata. Or maybe I could, but then it would become something other than Bach. With architecture, I can't just discard the structural calculations for a foundation and doodle my own geotechnical assumptions. A well-built castle isn't constructed on sand.

Is there room for speed in architecture? How about intuition?

Social psychologist David Sudnow comments on jazz as moving "from no one place in particular to no one place in particular." I wish architecture had this kind of freedom.

Some architects from the past, such as Spain's Antoni Gaudí, father of "Catalan Modernism" (there it is again, a label of style), created a world that may not necessarily be jazz-like but was certainly driven by fantastic personal, even randomly improvised, visions of the world.

Though his work was often based in structural engineering, Gaudí seemed free to explore, to break the rules, to create intuitively and work nonmethodically, like a modern sculptor or jazz pianist.

Gaudí was more than an architect influenced by a western civilization class on art history. He invented his own reality and techniques through an individualized perception driven by vast interests in ironwork, plaster treatments, carpentry, stained glass, and ceramics as well as Islamic-Hispanic arts, Gothic Revival, and the Industrial Revolution. With his enthusiasm for Romanticism and organic forms found in nature, there is no surprise that some describe his work as "lyrical."

I don't know if Gaudí liked jazz, but he appears to have practiced his art form in such a way that the resulting buildings are improvisational, inventive, spontaneous, and instinctive. Unlike what my colleagues and I do day after day, buried under client change requests, limited budgets, the details of a restaurant's exhaust fan, or the rainwater requirements for a new community, Antoni Gaudí approached architecture as if it were jazz.

As an architect, I can't spontaneously mold a chunk of clay around glass mosaic and say to clients and staff, "Here you are, your new university library. I just whipped this up for you."

Though I can't actually be like a jazz pianist playing improvisationally, I still try. I attempt to draw ideas freely without the constraints of either a T-square or the slow-to-reboot laptop. Later, I can worry about the PSI of a self-closing fire door. Rather than picking the best shade of red from the Pantone color book, I use my markers and color pencils, swiftly and even blindly, grabbing colors in a mad flurry of blended vibrant hues to create a color of the moment.

Akin to a jazz ensemble, my design team intentionally assembles without preconceived notions of a new project, without the design parameters of a city's constantly changing zoning codes, and definitely without the client's detailed twenty-two-page e-mail that specifies fifty-two square feet for a walk-in closet complete with seven-drawer dresser for ties and watches. The Poon Design team comes together without ego (okay, a little ego) or preference. We debate, draw, and play to see where we end up.

This collaborative approach is much more like jazz

than the methodology of many traditional corporations, where an executive draws up architectural ideas in the vacuum of his private office and has a senior project architect develop them for a presentation. After a closed-door meeting, the design team receives specific instructions, to be balanced with limiting city codes and mundane restrictions like delivery lead times for construction materials.

Though rational and logical, I doubt this structured corporate approach will ever produce a building as striking as Gaudí's church for the Sagrada Família, one of the most famous works of architecture in history, still under construction after a hundred years. As I said, architecture is slow. Tragically so.

 JAZZ AND JUXTAPOSITION—TWO words I might use to describe my work, my style regarding process and product. Very likely, I will replace these two words with two or three different words the next time an interviewer asks me, "What is your style?"

As architects have warned against, do I want to describe my style only to have someone assert that my work is nothing like jazz, in no way representative of juxtaposition?

Or as some architects proudly do, I could promote

myself through a witty brand label or slogan. Options: Eclectic Contemporary, Ironic Modernism, Organic Classicist, Structural Humorist, Colorful Minimalism, Nonrepresentational Dadaism, or Abstract Neorococo. How to choose?

I continue to work day by day. My personal interests drive my work. My private view of how people might interact in and with this glorious world influences what I draw each week. My various design teams of young and old architects, of engineers and collaborators, debate my ideas and generate strategies. At Poon Design, the best idea might not necessarily come from me. Together, we transform ideas into worthwhile designs.

In the end, I leave the labeling of our work to the media, writers, historians, colleagues, professors, critics, and fans. When I am long gone, I hope my design legacy is given an interesting designation of style.

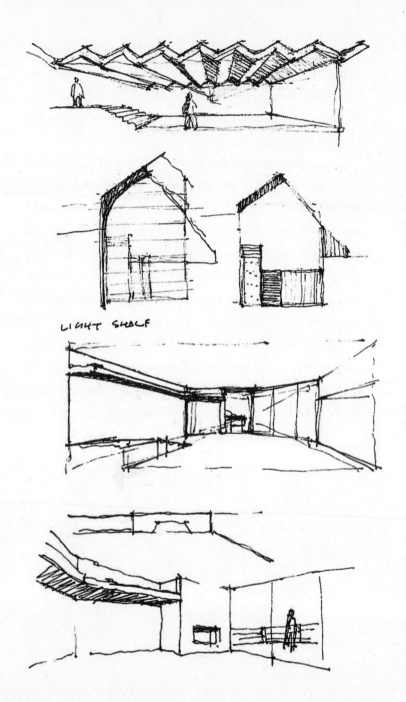

LIGHT SHELF

TEN THOUGHTS

OVER THE YEARS, I've incorporated the following thoughts into my design processes, into all my design work. In the middle of a design and its production, it can be easy to get lost in the pragmatics of the project: permits and approvals, function, budget, schedule, future maintenance, and constructability. In fact, as simple or even formulaic as it sounds, my notes can apply to many other pursuits, from fashion to website design, from gardening to music—and perhaps even to day-to-day existence.

1. Color. Color makes surfaces recede or stand out. Color can, by turn, soothe and enliven.

2. Light. Luminosity and light source, natural or artificial, push a static environment into motion.

3. Texture. Texture gives the hand something to touch and the eye something to process, from both far and near.

4. Pattern. Surroundings should have pace and tempo. Rhythm isn't just for music.

5. Scale. Grand scale is heroic. Small scale is intimate. Choose the right scale for the right activity.

6. Craft. A thoughtful, well-constructed project will last a lifetime and even change in meaning over time.

7. Humor. Can architecture have wit, irony, and charm? I think so.

8. Surprise. Unexpected moments deliver flair and amazement. Predictable architecture is boring.

9. Courage. Dream, and do not be timid. At times it might take some guts to get results.

10. Pleasure. At the end, good design should challenge and please, should bring delight, joy, and satisfaction.

part three

ARCHITECTURE FROM THE INSIDE

NORTH ELEVATION
1/16" = 1'-0"
12/14/05

THE MUSIC OF DESIGN

Music is liquid architecture.
Architecture is frozen music.

JOHANN WOLFGANG VON GOETHE

MY CONCEPT SKETCH on the left shows a public school exterior I designed and a piece of music that moves and flows as do the brick and glass of the building. They are separate and distinct creations, but purposeful in their own ways.

Music and architecture are the two languages through which I can speak to an audience. Whether playing a short piece by Chopin for a friend or designing a building, I am framing a story—whether for a solitary soul or for hundreds.

The performance of any work of music is steeped in interpretation—for both the creator and the listener—and so it is for architecture. A civic center, hospital, or park may be fully constructed as a physical environment, seemingly complete, but each will be visited and interpreted over and over again in many different ways. Architecture is open-ended, even incomplete. As the empty vessel of a museum wing is filled with the latest installations, it changes. One room of a house might begin as a family room, but its final function may never be final, as a family evolves with each chapter of their existence.

With music, the listener is given the privilege to engage the work and possibly declare it something quite different from the creator's intentions. So it is with design and architecture; the visitor decides what senses are influenced to what degree. As culture critic William Day writes, "Whatever is expressed in art leaves something unexpressed, and it is that which charms the imagination."

Except for dance and performance art, most art springs from the creator's mind and is immediately captured on paper or canvas—and none more so than music and architecture, which have additional unique parallels. Both have a defined structure.

Music and performing art are a bit more pliable, but are still more structured than we think. We can tell when two dancers are out of step, when the drummer is a beat behind. The painter and writer have rules as well, but their structures are far more subjective and free-ranging.

For architecture and musical composition, the prescribed spaces between beams and notes, the welding and the wavelengths, are highly defined by the statutes of science and mathematics. To defy gravity, or arguably the beat of music, may cause the structure to fail or fall.

 ONCE THE BASIC structural integrity of the composition or building is satisfied, the musician and builder have free rein to create complex and contradictory variations on the theme. Visually and aurally pleasing enhancements and embellishments set the song and the building apart from others. Melody, rhythm, and harmonies; arches, windows, and roofline. Instruments of the symphony; tile, wood, or stone for the library. Both have patterns and repetition; a baseline with repeating lyrical motifs.

The musical term *con moto* means "movement." Architects seek to create visual movement with lighting, the curve of a staircase, and the height of columns. It's all from the same creative palette. The Renaissance great Leon Battista Alberti said, "Characteristics that please the eye, also please the ear." Musical notes are sometimes seen as colors; colors of materials can be used as visual notes on a building surface.

I've been speaking here with mostly the overview in mind, but of course, musical composition and architectural design inhabit the inner core of every creation. Even Gehry's wild metal shapes are underpinned by exacting, scientifically grounded support, and a free-form jazz solo or blues guitar break returns to the original song structure at some point after soaring moments of variations on the theme. Symphonies have interludes, gentler moments in the whole when the interior composition plays off the larger theme.

Likewise, architects take larger design elements and develop them in intimate detail, or vice versa, and create quiet spaces to counterbalance grander gestures. Yes, the composer and architect can and do choose to shake us up with discordant notes and jarring spaces. The composer brings the disparate pieces of an epic symphony or opera back into compositional balance, and an architect ties together a complex collection of features that carry across a campus of buildings.

It is time to note the end to my metaphor about music and architecture on several levels, notably ground level. I can play the music, if I so choose, but I have not personally troweled a mound of concrete or wielded a spot welder. The architect must turn over his work to skilled hands. I make the marks on paper, but I need others to see my work through. The music I have written is both a moment of personal creation and carrying out of the action, but my design life entails an inevitable moment of departure. I must also reconcile my idealistic agenda with the demands of budget, schedule, and municipal codes. My work is a servant to gravity, the limited resources of the earth, and the furies of Mother Nature.

One more thing to temper the feeling of elation when I make my first sketch of a new building. As with years of practicing music, for an architect, the road to career success, if there is such a thing, is measured by the milestones of apprenticeships and bad jobs, rejected projects and government bureaucracy, failures and egos. I don't mean to complain too much. One learns to develop a thick skin, like the calluses on a guitarist's fingertips. We are both no less fulfilled, and the goal in both arts—all arts—is in the enjoyment of the recipient.

I have enjoyed my journey as a musician and an architect. I enjoy that both endeavors have rules, from the law of gravity to the principles of sound waves. I like to embrace the rules, create within the rules, and then break them.

With over 150 completed projects, large and small, and many more in mind, I still vividly remember how I almost took a different course. Periodically, I still wonder if architecture is right for me. After all, music had been my first love all along. Was it a mistake that I eventually chose to draw boundaries on large sheets of architectural paper instead of writing notes on the five lines of staff paper?

 I HAD SPENT two decades of my life practicing piano, composing music, studying composers and their theories, and performing in recitals and concerts. My goal was to be a concert pianist, not an architect, but I also realized that the odds in favor of a viable professional career as a musician were slim.

 I GRADUATED CAL Berkeley with a B.A., magna cum laude, having studied architecture and music, and off I went to explore life in New York City for a while.

One very late night in my Chelsea studio apartment in 1987, I clenched two graduate school applications in my hands: one for the Juilliard School of Music and the other for Harvard's Graduate School of Design.

As I pondered how many concert pianists existed in the universe, I named Rubinstein, Horowitz, Ashkenazy, Arrau, Serkin, and many more. In the end, the list was actually short—and I had to reach far into history to populate the list. I hypothesized that although there were only a handful of classical pianists in the world, there were hundreds and perhaps thousands of successful architects in every city. In addition, I figured that I could not be a thriving concert pianist and operate an architecture business. But I could be a practicing architect *and* still practice music.

I chose architecture, and my place in this discipline sustains me to this day. I made a first choice, one that didn't negate all others. I still play the piano nearly every day, whether a small bit of Brahms and Bach, an intimate session of improvisation, or *Cinderella* for my young daughters to sing and dance along with.

Since one never forgets one's first love, I've made it a point to seek out commissions for art spaces, theaters, and classrooms—structures in which young and old can sing, dance, read, and draw, and where they, like me, can learn which path(s) they might follow.

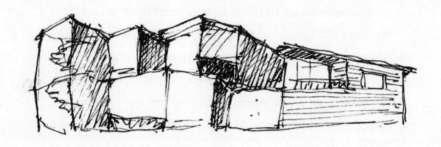

8/28/07 CAR WASH NEG.

ONE BALCONY ?

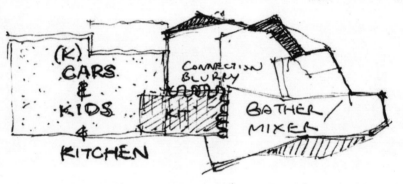

(K)
CARS
&
KIDS
&
KITCHEN

CONNECTION
BLURRY

KIT

BATHER /
MIXER

PRIVATE · BEDROOM
CAR · GARAGE
PRES · KIT
STATIC · STOR

POWDER
LIVING   } ENTERTAIN
DINING
MASTER · PRIVATE
STAIR · MOTION

CARS & KIDS
FRESH & HIP
TO SOMETHING
OLD

OLDER · CRINKLY &
WRINKLY
TO SOMETHING
NEW

START STRAIGHT → CONFUSED

THE LOST ART OF LETTERING

*An ounce of practice is worth more than
tons of preaching.*

GANDHI

THERE ARE DYING art forms—and there are dead art forms.

Before computers became the norm in the production of architectural drawings, architects annotated their handmade drawings with a distinctive style of writing known as lettering. It was not *just* writing; it was *lettering*.

At my first internship, I spent four hours a day just learning to handwrite letters and numbers on designs properly, all in preparation for final blueprinting. It was an integral part of every architect's day. Lettering by hand was endlessly practiced and honed to perfection like other, more artistic art forms. Lettering was taught, learned, and refined, akin to a concert pianist practicing scales. The goal was absolute precision.

The purpose of lettering was not grandiose; it was

merely meant to communicate and explain. But the beauty, consistency, integrity, and conviction with which lettering was executed made it transcend any form of mere cursive or script. In its day, lettering was architectural calligraphy.

An architect might letter information such as the dimensions of a doorway, the material to be used for a wall, or the angle of a sloped roof. Lettering was always written entirely in upper case and in a blocky, squareish, formal style. Of course, lettering was done all by hand, painstakingly and carefully, stroke by stroke, using many different tools of the trade: a mechanical pencil or lead holder, a triangle, T-square, templates, and sandpaper to create the perfect point.

Architectural offices issued graphic standards on how lettering was to be done specific to that firm. Standards included the exact height of letters and numbers, the acceptable slope and swerve of Q and R, 7 and 8, and even what lead graphite to use.

The harder the lead, the more precise the line, but there was the trap and possibility of frequently breaking the tip of your pencil point, an edge chiseled, then smoothed using sandpaper. *Too* sharp and you were in danger of cutting through the delicate tracing paper or of the figures not coming out dark and clear enough during the ensuing blueprinting stage.

Though this may sound trivial and neurotic to a

modern ear, office standards were established to ensure that if several architects were working on the same set of drawings, the lettering would be consistent, uniform, professional, and readable at the construction site. Be they conceptual ideas or construction requirements, clarity was key. It's lovely to get the commission, with your glorious creation taking your client's breath away, but all is for naught if the builder can't read the road map for the structure.

Think of the subcontractor at the site ready to pour concrete into a form or plaster a curved wall. The drawings are dirty and wrinkled from the days and weeks in a busy construction environment. The contractor cannot waste time interpreting—or worse, misinterpreting—an architect's personal cursive to figure out if the correct dimensions are 5 or 50 inches or feet by 20 or 200 feet. The. Information. Must. Be. Clear. From one professional to another, the transmitted information must be the diametric opposite of a doctor's RX scrawl.

Here's a surprise.

Architects, instructed to follow office standards, studiously hunched over their sketches of rooms and roof lines, are contrary. Very contrary. In this ambitious world of competition, ego, and excellence, every architect with an individual flair—which is all of us—consistently undermines the goal of consistency. Though every architect in the days of lettering was trained to have a standard of lettering, he or she also sought to express a subtle and unique variation on the approved lettering that carefully undermined the office standards without obliterating them.

At some firms, this paradox led to great battles of artistic and management egos: establishing standards, enforcing them, subverting them, deflecting them, and honoring them.

FORTUNATELY, LETTERING PEACE reigned in one of my first jobs. Early in my career, I apprenticed with San Francisco's Robert Swatt, the founder of an intimate creative firm. When I started, there were four staff members: Swatt and his wife plus a project architect and his girlfriend. Despite the modest setting and spatial intimacy—a one-room, bare, industrial office—Swatt Architects produced some of the most exquisite homes and commercial projects of its time, creating a cool California Modernism using classic and warm materials. Many decades later, I am still in touch with Robert and consider him a mentor.

As an apprentice, I held many entry-level job responsibilities, from drafting to measuring, from site visits to graphic design. Of course, I was also intensely trained to letter. I learned what is so quickly identified as this architect's style of lettering. It's an individual typeface, if you will, that is not copyrighted or intellectual property, and it's passed on as a modest but important craft from mentor to apprentice.

On certain days, I practiced my lettering for hours on end, carefully using my T-square to ensure that all vertical strokes, like the start of the letter E, were perfectly vertical, and the horizontal strokes were broader than the vertical, using the aforementioned chisel-edged pencil shaped with sandpaper of the proper grit. In addition to consistency, speed was paramount in a small shop, and through years of practice, I eventually attained both.

 WITH THE ARRIVAL of the computer, the art of lettering faded with little fanfare. Why take hours of a day to lovingly hand letter when a keyboard is faster, more efficient, easier to correct, and crystal clear in its instructions to contractors?

Some traditions do die hard, however. For a short transition period from the art of the hand to digital technology, computer software programs such as Auto-CAD and Microsoft Word offered fonts like "Architect's Typeface" or "The Draftsman." There were even computer fonts that were based on a specific architect's personal style of lettering, notably Frank Lloyd Wright and Richard Neutra; both were giants in the arts of drawing and lettering.

These programs used the technology of the computer to provide a font that was supposed to look like it did *not* come from a computer. The most sophisticated versions built in random details and variations so as to give the computer font the look and feel of handcrafted and handwritten lettering.

But in the end, such a technological approach to replicate an architect's hand lettering was an act of holding on, perhaps even grieving. And the fabricated architect-style computer typefaces vanished quickly. Saving time won the day, as is the way of many things. Periodically, you will find an architect still hand lettering his annotations on a drawing, or perhaps just creating a project title block in the artisanal way. The visual impact is invariably artful and warm. Aside from the visual effect, this use of lettering in a few places—I still hand letter if I have the time and inclination—speaks to a lost world of authenticity, preparation, and beauty. These days, lettering seems slow and time consuming, but that is the point.

Lettering *is* slow and disciplined.

The art of lettering embraced patience, rigor, composure, and grace. The modest act of writing each individual letter by hand is still an act of immense care and poise.

HERE'S ANOTHER SURPRISE. Or perhaps not. As the expression goes, "Nostalgia isn't what it used to be." There were several silly and some truly awful aspects of the world of lettering for a blueprint.

As the sculptor of yore inhaled marble dust and the glass blower filled his lungs with heat and dust, beginning architects endured a lung bath of ammonia. Old-style blueprint paper was coated entirely in ammonium iron, the light-sensitive sheets stored in large flat files in darkrooms where management sent young architects to be sacrificed. Occupying an entire wall, blueprinting machines were approached with caution. In every studio, the machine hummed and flashed lights in accompaniment to the deafening reverberation of the barely adequate ventilation system, like some rigged-up machine in a bad sci-fi movie.

You had to carefully set your original drawing on top of a bright yellow sheet, then feed them both into the blueprint machine, in perfect alignment, with perfect timing. The hazards were many: stuck finger or caught sleeve, misaligned sheets or a print setting that was too dark or too light. Or the evil machine could just destroy the original drawing—crinkling it, tearing it, or simply getting jammed and ruining it. And the original could contain a hundred hours of drawing time.

Though the possibilities were grim, there was a satisfaction of getting that perfectly aligned print with the right contrast on the first try, and doing so was outright demanded by the bosses. The machines and electric power were not to be wasted on a young architect trying to learn through trial and error. We newbies, eyes filled with tears and brain cells falling by the wayside, were the ones who had to endure this ammonia-filled cell.

 AMMONIA FUMES NOTWITHSTANDING, I stubbornly and absurdly tend to romanticize the tools and craft of making a blueprint. Still, some aspects of blueprinting and the art of lettering seem completely ridiculous now. I remember an arcane product called Pounce, a mysterious coarse white powder. Architects would apply the Pounce, shaking it out onto a 30-by-42-inch blank sheet of paper from what looked like a giant saltshaker. It was an odd spectacle. One end of the Pounce dispenser had a white felt edge, which was used to smooth out the distribution of this powder across the paper. The powder was supposed to keep the drawing clean as one's T-square, rulers, and triangles were dragged across the graphite-covered surface. If the architect chose to draw with an ink pen, Pounce was supposed to make the drawing surface more absorbent so as to take the ink, making a crisp and sharp drawing.

I found the overall practice of using Pounce bizarre and, worse, counterproductive. It never made the drawing clean; rather, it just smudged the graphite around in messy clouds, and when the powder clumped up, it hindered the path of the pencil across the sheet of paper. As for ink, I found that Pounce made the surface uneven in absorption; in some areas, the ink would not be absorbed, and in other areas, the ink would swell in blobs.

A supposed advance came with the Mylar-based blueprint process. With that, however, came the medieval-sounding "Eradicator." Instead of blue, the resulting color was brown, and instead of paper, the reproduction was transferred onto a sheet of plastic. The goal of the sepia Mylar was to allow further work on the Mylar reproduction, like updating information or moving lines. But the sepia lines were too permanent to erase with a regular eraser.

Enter the Eradicator, a form of a chemical eraser, a bleach-like liquid in a small bottle that was applied with a small brush. With the goal of erasing the mistake and allowing the drawing area to be redrawn, the result only looked like the mistake it was: a bleached-out surface with new work done with a black-lead pencil that, unlike graphite pencil lead, would adhere to the Mylar—standing out from the sepia lines like sweatpants under a tux jacket.

The only "benefit" I could see from all this was that a

senior architect could now enjoy the delightful scent of ammonia otherwise reserved for the junior staff in the blueprint room.

 TODAY, DIGITAL SCANNING, large-scale inkjet and laser printers, and drafting software have replaced blue and sepia printing. All that *has* made life a lot easier. But a niche group of architects, typically of a previous generation such as me, continue to practice with fervor and loyalty the methods of a world gone by. For me, it is akin to the care and joy of handling a vinyl LP record album: cleaning it, placing it on the turntable platter, watching the tone arm gracefully swing over and down, and . . . music. Not downloaded from the cloud, which is just a warehouse off a highway somewhere, but the tangible, tactile reproduction of music.

Is it nostalgic reminiscence or perhaps a commitment to a craft that keeps the tools of an old world around? Lettering is gone in 99 percent of architecture studios, but the fanatical pledge to hand lettering is so intense in the 1 percent that it might be confused with self-righteousness. It isn't. Some of us just miss the old world of architectural design and production. It was a craft. We had tools of the trade that became a part of our bodies and limbs, like an old catcher's mitt or a favorite pair of shoes. Our tools showed a wear and patina that were a signature, looking aged and rich.

Today, I'm happy to have my brain cells intact, and I spend the time that I used to spend lettering indulging myself in the lovely art of sketching ideas. And practicing my piano scales.

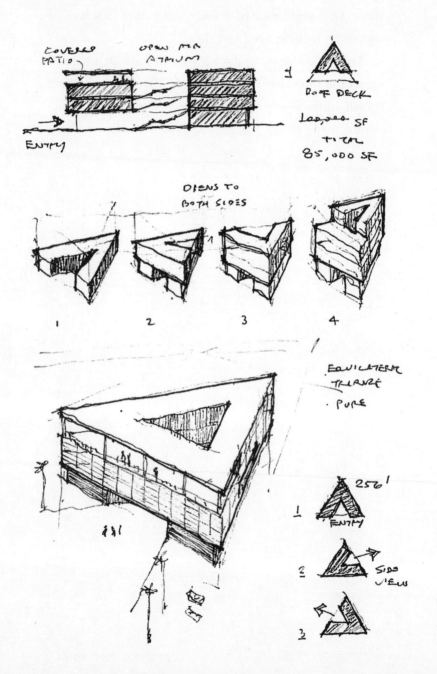

COVERED PATIO

OPEN AIR ATRIUM

ENTRY

ROOF DECK

100,000 SF
TOTAL
85,000 SF

OPENS TO BOTH SIDES

1   2   3   4

EQUILATERAL TRIANGLE
· PURE

256'

1 ENTRY

2 SIDE VIEW

3

THE SIX PHASES OF
ARCHITECTURE

Ah, to build, to build! That is the noblest
art of all the arts. Painting and sculpture are but
images, are merely shadows cast by outward things on
stone or canvas, having in themselves
no separate existence.
Architecture, existing in itself, and not in seeming
a something it is not, surpasses them as
substance shadow.

HENRY WADSWORTH LONGFELLOW

WHEN YOU HIRE an architect, you will likely run across the "phases" of the architectural process. These phases make up the creative journey from beginning to end and, though not necessarily linear, are common in practice. They are conventional as an industry standard as well as in contracts. Though each project is unique, this chapter outlines the six typical architectural phases:

1. Planning
2. Schematic Design
3. Design Development
4. Construction Documents
5. Bidding
6. Construction Administration

PLANNING

Planning your project is important. This phase—also called "predesign" or "programming"—defines your project in terms of approximate size, program, initial budget, and schedule.

As an example, if you are designing a house, you will be asked questions about such issues as how many bedrooms, how many bathrooms, one story or two, how many children, wine collection, home theater, gym, swimming pool, pets, etc.

As another example, if you are designing a school, consider how many students, traditional versus progressive teaching methods, school funding and schedule, technology, size of administration, food program, etc.

Discussions of design, style, materials, and colors come in later phases. The planning phase is about discovering who you are.

Whether designing a house, restaurant, arts building, or an entire college campus, typical tools of the architect for this phase involve charts of square footage and uses, conceptual physical models, site analysis illustrations, and concept sketches. Diagrams, often called "adjacency diagrams" or "bubble diagrams," are drawn, indicating what functions are next to each other, but without direction as to feel and character

SCHEMATIC DESIGN

This phase launches the design and artistic process. Ideas and dreams are explored. With you as client and collaborator, your architect will brainstorm and play.

Preliminary options that capture the general intent of your project are sketched out. This phase is fluid and dynamic, working to establish the design intent, a preliminary budget, and an approximate schedule. Back and forth—client to architect and architect to client— the personality and expression of your project are defined.

In this phase, it is important to capture the Big Ideas. During "roll-up-your-sleeve" meetings, your project is studied through floor plans, interior sketches, exterior views, and physical models. Architects should ask: What is the essence of your project?

DESIGN DEVELOPMENT

In this phase, ideas are refined: the relationship of project parts, the forms and shapes, sizes and square footages, materials, and details.

The Design Development phase also begins the technical explorations. The architect will work with engineers and consultants on structure, site infrastructure, and sustainability. Consultants typically include engineers for structural, mechanical, electrical, and plumbing engineering. Other consultants of design and technical expertise could include an audio-video consultant, security consultant, acoustician, landscape designer, interior decorator, and so on.

The architect ensures that the project is in compliance with building codes and agency requirements. Floor plans are developed technically and in greater detail. Refined through technical software as well as hand drawings, the process looks at many details from window heights to furniture position to stone cladding. The overall style and character of your project are further honed, exploring what this building will look and feel like.

CONSTRUCTION DOCUMENTS

This phase is focused on the constructability and permitting of your project. In coordination with engineers and consultants, the design team will produce your Construction Documents, a detailed set of drawings that demonstrates to the general contractor and the city agencies how the project will be executed.

These documents, a dozen or several hundred sheets, explain many aspects of the building, such as roof drainage, details for windows and doors, plumbing fixtures, building dimensions to a fraction of an inch, demolition information, and criteria for air quality.

At the conclusion of this phase, the Construction Documents are submitted for agency review and, hopefully, approval and a building permit.

BIDDING

Though there are various approaches to pricing, one common approach is to provide the Construction Documents to potential general contractors and request their proposed construction cost. The architect works with the client in negotiating the best balance between the design goals, the realities of cost, and the scope of work provided by the contractor. The result of the Bidding process is traditionally a contract, with a budget and schedule from a qualified contractor.

CONSTRUCTION ADMINISTRATION

With the general contractor on board, construction begins. On a regular basis, the architect observes construction and determines if the work meets the design intent of the Construction Documents. As unforeseen issues always arise, the architect attempts to resolve crises that result from the complicated reality that is construction.

THE ABOVE SIX phases can be shortened, combined, or expanded. Additional phases might include "post-occupancy" reviews, which are an assessment of how well the building has performed now that it is in use for a certain period of time.

Whether three phases or nine, understand that the industry of architecture has created structure and precedence to organize the creative process so that the journey is an enjoyable and a professional one.

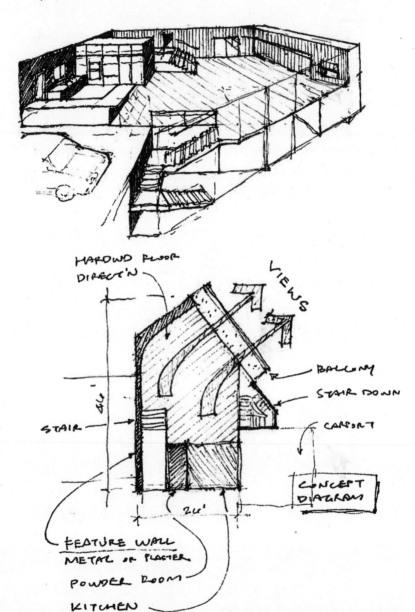

11/28/13 DANVILLE   1

HARDWD FLOOR
DIRECT'N

VIEWS

BALCONY

STAIR DOWN

CARPORT

STAIR

CONCEPT
DIAGRAM

FEATURE WALL
METAL or PLASTER

POWDER ROOM

KITCHEN

PERILS OF BEING
AN ARCHITECT

A doctor can bury his mistakes, but an architect can only advise his clients to plant vines.

FRANK LLOYD WRIGHT

ARCHITECTURE IS A tool that sets the stage for engaging experiences, such as in a church where natural light dramatically beams through narrow windows to cast shadows and colors changing and shifting throughout the day, months, and seasons. Less dramatic but no less enjoyable, architecture can also influence the atmosphere of social spaces, such as with welcoming and openhearted materials, details, and colors inspired by a chef's cuisine. Or, taking a different tack, architecture can be mute, like the design of a powerfully silent museum that serves as a backdrop for the work of artists.

Such is the beauty of architecture: the capacity and aptitude to define space and time, to offer uplifting or calming experiences. If the architect can create forms appropriate to each space; suppress his or her own ego; and employ abstract notions of composition, massing, proportion, and scale, the people who will inhabit the space will be moved by what's in it and perhaps not even be aware of the space itself.

As is our nature, architects do have egos, and we can't help but want our work to be seen—in the background, foreground, and all around! Consequently, we must remind ourselves of one basic rule of most structures: Architecture revolves around function and purpose, not solely form and beauty. In some cases, I'd even intone the doctor's oath: First, do no harm.

Architecture must have purpose and utility, first and foremost. A building may be a poetic expression of sculpture and material, but its most basic purpose is to provide shelter and safety in the most reliable method possible.

This purpose can be mundane at times.

The bathroom in my parents' house comes vividly to mind as an example. I have little criticism of the color of paint or the type of wall tile in said bathroom. I hold no grudge against the style of the countertop and mirrors. With anxiety bordering on anger, each time I enter the bathroom I am confronted by the (not me) designer's poor location of the light switches.

Why the drama?

When you enter this unfortunate bathroom, there are two light switches to the right of the doorway. One would expect one switch to turn on a ceiling or mirror light, but no. The first switch turns on a cheap ceiling vent that rattles loudly in the dark room. The second switch turns on a spotlight over the curtained shower. Great. The most functional light switch is several steps across the dark room. Under the mirror. Near the sink. In a hard-to-reach corner.

Architecture is vexing when it has failed. Regardless of the charming side window over the tub that captures the view of the trees, and no matter how well the patterned wall covering complements the artwork over the toilet, the bathroom just doesn't work. The architecture falls on its face upon the first step into the room.

Bathrooms aside, we have all experienced kitchen layouts that don't allow the refrigerator door to open fully, restaurant tables that get blasted by cold air whenever someone enters, and public buildings with hallways to nowhere.

Daily annoyances aside, architecture *can* do harm.

ARCHITECTURE CAN FAIL catastrophically. Consider a movie theater with inadequate exit lighting and doors or a transit terminal with poor public address or monitoring technology. What if an architect specified the wrong kind of flooring for a school hallway, and a student slipped and fell? The architect is supposed to understand the slip resistance of flooring products—particularly in public spaces—from porcelain tile to concrete finishes to polished terrazzo to granite pavers.

The perils of being an architect go far beyond whether she or he has successfully created a world of splendor within an environment of function. The risks lie in our responsibility to what is known officially in the industry as "health, safety and welfare." Whether it is a design of an apartment kitchen or a convention center, the architect takes on the responsibility of protecting the inhabitants by providing a safe and sane environment.

Though this may sound righteous and grandiose, the skill set acquired by an architect through many years of education and a rigorous state licensing test is nothing of the sort. It is essential. I consider my responsibility no different from that of a doctor prescribing medications or a lawyer advising a client. The depth of knowledge required of such professionals can be overwhelming and can overshadow the joys and rewards of being part of such professions.

In a true and dreadful story, the negligent actions of an architect actually killed someone. The charges brought against the architect? Involuntary manslaughter.

In 2011, a fire occurred at a Los Angeles home designed by this architect. During the fire, the ceiling failed, collapsing on and killing a firefighter while injuring eleven others. The ensuing investigation determined that the flames began in a negligently installed fireplace. It was also questioned whether the ceiling and sprinkler system were appropriately designed.

The architect pleaded no contest in 2013, was found guilty, and will serve up to four years in prison. The house was originally considered beautiful enough to be featured on a television show; the beauty of the architecture trumped proper and safe functionality.

While I often rail against the tiny minds of the regulating agencies, I am reminded, when I see news of horrible devastation that earthquakes wreak on poorly built homes, of the need for absolute quality and care when building *anything.*

IN MOST CASES, mistakes that an architect might make can be resolved ahead of time. As part of the design process, a quality-control team in an architect's office carefully reviews *all* of the drawings created for any project, from new balconies for a hotel to the correct slope of a ramp for wheelchair access. No such items are as glamorous as capturing that heavenly church sunlight, but the basics—every detail— are critical to the success of architecture overall and to the safety of its users.

I would guess an architect spends 20 percent of his energy on the creative side, the side that the world seems to know, honor, and romanticize. The remaining 80 percent is focused on the details. Carefully, precisely worked through with as much love and care as the overall vision.

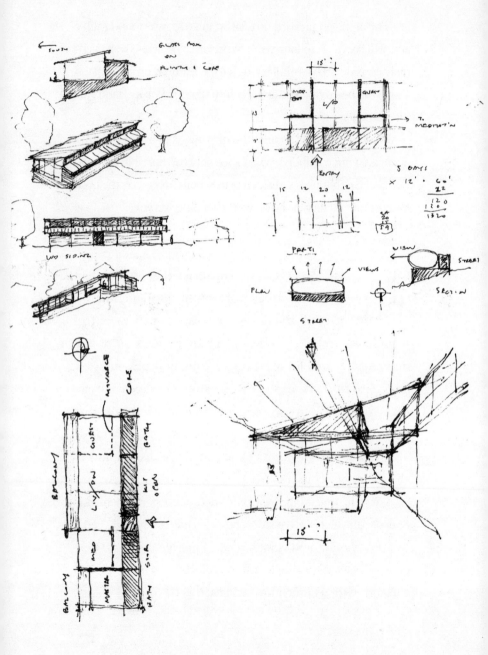

REASONS FOR AN ARCHITECT

*The ancient Romans built their greatest
masterpieces of architecture, their amphitheaters,
for wild beasts to fight in.*

VOLTAIRE

I OFTEN WONDER why anyone would voluntarily hire an architect and partake in the architectural creative process. The journey from idea to construction can be painful and treacherous. As soon as our design and construction process begins, it seems like all architects ever do is put out fires and avoid daily catastrophes.

Why would a client want to go through the exhausting process of vetting architects, interviewing them and hearing the same pitches, only to then proceed with endless design meetings about the cascading limits of budget and schedule on one's expectations? Why would a client trail along as the architect daily coordinates the engineers, suppliers, contractors, and inspectors?

Months pass, and there is not yet an actual physical

new residence, new corporate headquarters, or shopping center but rather a stack of computerized abstract lines and numbers on large sheets of paper. This information is supposed to magically represent your dream building so that a general contractor can someday build said structure for you—and with fingers crossed, it will all work out fine.

Then it gets worse. The project requires approval from the Department of Building and Safety, from the Department of Planning and Zoning, from the Planning Commission, from endless design review boards and public hearings that reject and gut every exciting aspect of your project. This process alone takes a few months, or even several years.

For one of our Beverly Hills clients, the city approval process took ten times longer than normal. The city planners demanded that our project include parking on the premises. This was physically impossible, since the lot size was merely one thousand square feet, not large enough to include any form of adjacent or underground garage, ramp-to-rooftop parking, or street-level parking. We challenged this requirement, citing the laws of physics—you cannot put a watermelon in a box the size of an acorn.

Though we won this battle, and the requirement was waived after the planners saw the absurdity of their request—to force a potato inside an egg—it took over a year of debate, presentations, meetings, and phone calls. During this time, our client unfortunately paid monthly rent on a prestigious piece of real estate. She wasted hundreds of thousands of dollars on an empty space while we waited for the city to grant a permit to start construction. The only small justice was that the city planner was fired for pursuing such a nonsensical requirement.

Why would any client want to go through such drama and trauma as well as financial loss? After barely surviving such a convoluted permitting process, the construction of a project can be even more painful, as every phase comes in over budget or is behind schedule, the city inspectors change their minds from day to day, and the project seems to go on for months or years without ever taking shape.

Here is the thing: The pure joy of having your own custom-designed home, your own perfectly tailored law office, office building, church, or any other building, big or small, that expresses your vision and personality— well, such a delight cannot be captured in simple words. The joy of seeing your vision develop into an office tower among others in the skyline, into a museum ideal for sharing your art collection, or into a specialty hospital is a triumph unlike anything else.

The architectural journey may produce many obstacles and much anguish during design, permitting, and construction, but when finally completed, the opening of your project will more than compensate for the many challenges that arose throughout the process.

A friend once compared the emotional undertaking of pregnancy to the architectural process. Silly? Yes, but let me explain.

In the beginning, everything is a celebration. During the middle, it might be great, but it might also be difficult. Toward the end, the mother screams for relief and might exclaim, "Get this alien out of my body." After delivery, the last painful period passes so quickly from the mother's memory that another pregnancy is contemplated even within months of the delivery. Though the pregnancy involved many months of confusion, anguish, and worry, most mothers would state with little hesitation that the end result was well worth it and that the joy cannot easily be captured by words.

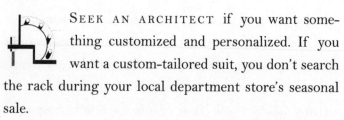 SEEK AN ARCHITECT if you want something customized and personalized. If you want a custom-tailored suit, you don't search the rack during your local department store's seasonal sale.

Hire an architect if you want something special, something individualized, something that captures a character, expression, and personality that is exclusive to you or your institution. It might be uniquely part of the educational methodology for your school, or a distinct part of your experiential brand of service for your retail center.

Architects are here to usher a dream into reality. It could be as small as a simple interior concept for a café in the perfect combination of the flooring material, display shelving, and adjustable lighting, or it could be as complex as a new museum such as the Guggenheim Museum in New York City.

Architects are here to listen to the most detailed of scenarios and concepts. I have heard a wife speak for hours about growing up thinking the best sunlight dapples in through lace curtains, as she tucked her small self into a window bay to read one of her favorite novels. I have read a client's fifty-page treatise on how his estate would function, including the top dresser drawer that would be lined in brown velvet and store his fifty-piece cufflink collection.

Architects, if we are fortunate to be hired by you, synthesize all this information and provide you with the joy of dreams realized and the satisfaction of expectations met.

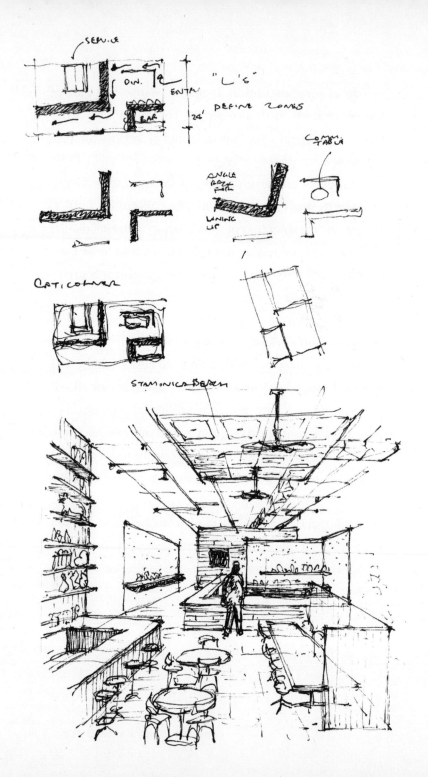

IT TAKES MORE THAN

ONE ARCHITECT

Good design goes to heaven; bad design goes everywhere.

MIEKE GERRITZEN

IT WOULD BE fantastic if I could brag that all of the creative work by Poon Design was mine and only mine, that I am the sole genius responsible for all of our creations. This pompous sentiment would support my ego and contribute to my delusions of grandeur about being a rock star or the next Michelangelo. Such a statement would be grossly misleading.

The media enjoys supporting tales like that of Frank Lloyd Wright or the fictional Howard Roark as solo artistic visionaries. The headlines are exciting, easy to grasp, and readily digestible by the mass population: "I. M. Pei Adds Glass Pyramid to the Louvre," or "With Disney Concert Hall, Frank Gehry Creates Masterpiece."

Similarly, with George Lucas's *Star Wars* or Martha Stewart's paint colors, if one believes a single hand brought you such greatness, then one has to ask what the hundreds of people in the offices of Pei, Gehry, Lucas, and Stewart are doing.

The studio of Poon Design boasts many individuals with diverse talents, interests, and abilities. At the most basic level, my job as founder and president of this company entails building the artistic machine that designs greatness.

I seek out, employ, and inspire the team of talent, author the primary creative themes that propel a project, create the hierarchy of ideas and the process that supports it, guide the team day by day, edit the work week by week, and assemble managerial pieces.

Then I pray that it all clicks together, and the team raises my initial ideas to a higher level. Like a film director, a restaurant chef, or a symphony conductor, my role is to guide and direct. Yes, I create, form, generate, invent, and produce, but I do so with the team that is Poon Design.

Though the solo artist is overly romanticized, know that the atelier structure is commonplace throughout most creative industries. Every architecture office is made up of teams of people, just as every symphony is made up of musicians from violinist to flutist to timpani player.

COMPLEMENTARY, COLLABORATIVE, AND integrated expertise makes up my studio. The summaries that follow are not job descriptions but simply what the organization has evolved into over the decades.

The team always has a senior architect, an expert authority who has over fifty years of professional experience practicing architecture around the globe. This senior architect is the voice of reason and experience, a quintessential professional often thought to be from another epoch, different from the ragtag assembly of youthful energy. Our senior architect is a designer of exquisite taste as well as a practiced moderator of client politics.

When this architect draws a front door, for example, it is of perfect proportion and detail. When he challenges a client, it is to raise the project's artistry to a sublime level, and this architect does so without bruising a client's ego.

Poon Design's director of architecture is a separate individual from the senior architect. The director is responsible for the development, progression, and maturation of a design, whether it begins as a loose conceptual sketch, a cardboard model, or a series of preliminary design drawings created on the computer. The director advances ideas toward the real structure of a building. He balances the creative agenda with realities such as budget, schedule, building codes, and construction details.

If a project contains a wild, sculpturally shaped roof, for example, sketched by me on a piece of scrap paper in a flurry of impatience, then this director of architecture not only makes the roof shape into a physical reality that adheres to the laws of engineering, but he also ensures that the roof will not leak.

These two architects lead a team of midlevel architects who work furiously to make a project into reality, toiling day by day. The work of this production team requires a wide range of skills and activities from computer drafting to computer modeling, from specifying the exact stain for a wood window frame to the exact tint of colored glass that this frame will hold.

Supporting both the executive team and the production team are youthful apprentice architects who work for days without sleep for the sake of being part of this exciting industry. Coming from the top of their graduating classes, these young men and women execute the most poetic and potent of exercises while also performing the most mundane and routine.

On a humdrum day, they answer phones, take meeting minutes, organize the library of stone samples, and arrange the vendor catalogs in alphabetical order.

On other days, they sketch inventive ideas that inspire the entire office, construct physical models of paper and glue that drive a project toward the final, beautiful result, and witness firsthand all aspects of the project—of *their* project.

The Poon Design team includes other specialists and experts. To architecture's three-dimensional world, our graphic designers add their two-dimensional vision. The graphic designers develop aspects separate from architecture but inherent to the identity and character of a client's project.

Items include business cards, menus, matchbook covers, packaging, to-go bags, coffee cups, wine lists, websites, event invitations, freeway billboards, and magazine/online advertisements. For one bakery client, we designed not only the logo but also their presentation box. We engineered how the opening, closing, and locking of the box would best present the baked goods while also allowing the goods to be transported safely.

Our landscape designer collaborates with all the architects to create natural surroundings that serve a project. Her designs go beyond selecting flowers, though assembling scent, colors, and textures is indeed an art form. Besides the obvious of designing pavers, exterior lighting, gates, walls, benches, trellises, fences, fountains, fire pits, barbecues, and even cabanas, the work also includes the technical side: irrigation, waterproofing, drainage, electrical engineering, seasonal and solar exposure, wind control, and drought tolerance.

Many of our architects are interior designers and decorators as well. For some offices of limited services and imagination, of which there are many, the staff merely designs the shell of the building. They must turn their project over to an interior design company to flesh out the rest of the vision.

For Poon Design, the ideas that drive the design of a building are powerful enough to direct not just the shaping of a building but completion of the entire interior, from materials to finishes to colors, textures, furnishings, and art. Exterior and interior design at Poon Design are never separate.

Our interior prowess includes the design of furniture, cabinetry, lighting fixtures, and so on, including the lines, materials, and methods of fabrication, such as milled, water-jet cut, laser cut, or sawed by hand.

Our lighting designer brings our architecture to life. By illuminating surfaces, adding halos and glows, bouncing shadows, manipulating colors, and enhancing surfaces, our architecture becomes a showcase of brightness and revelation, a romantic mystery, or a haunted and enigmatic tale.

 EVERY TEAM MEMBER of Poon Design is more than a single-track designer. We have architects who are photographers, writers, musicians, painters, sculptors, product designers, industrial designers, poets, athletes, world travelers, and teachers. We have individuals who are car mechanics and chefs. One is an aeronautical engineer. Yes, a rocket scientist.

I believe not just in collaboration but in cross-pollination. The alliance between our interests and abilities under the umbrella of architecture offers the most innovative thinking. It is this kind of architecture that not only allows me the luxury of saying that we design everything but also makes such a heroic ambition truthful.

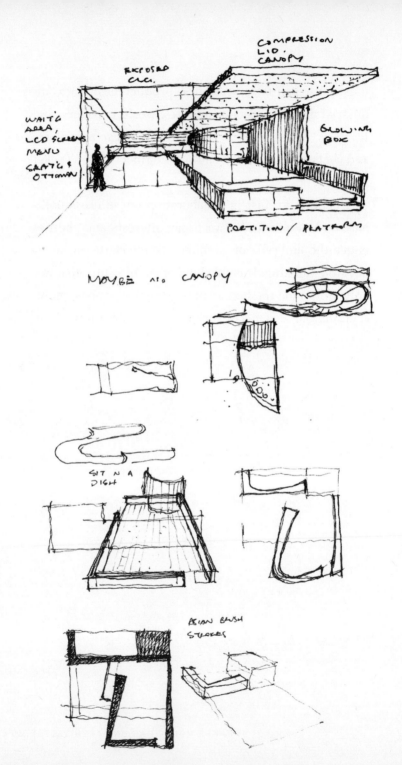

COMPRESSION
LID
CANOPY

EXPOSED
CIRC.

WAIT'G
AREA,
LCD SCREENS
MENU
SEAT'G &
OTTOMAN

GROWING
BOX

PARTITION / PLATFORM

MAYBE NO CANOPY

SIT N A
DISH

ASIAN BRUSH
STROKES

WITH PEN AND PAPER

Architecture is the reaching out for the truth.

LOUIS KAHN

WITH PEN AND paper, I can shape the world.

Architecture is a stimulating and diverse field of practice for me. Though I sought to be a classical pianist and at one time became moderately accomplished, being an architect allows for involvement in a service industry while honing my skills in creation. Not as pure an art form as a Mozart piano sonata, architecture takes on many forms, the complexities and contradictions of striving toward social good and the progress of our civilization.

When one considers that architecture includes museums, bridges, churches, schools, community centers, parks, gardens, libraries, memorials, commerce, sports, entertainment, parking structures, and communications as well as domesticity, family life, and a home, it becomes clear that architecture is everything that is designed, developed, and constructed around you.

Architecture is both the blank canvas that provides for the imprint of your life and the vessel that holds it.

When I performed music, I shared a form of virtuoso art that I practiced with discipline and passion. Architecture is also such an art form. It is not spontaneous like poetry, for architecture requires a specific client such as an educational board, church committee, or homeowner. Architecture is not just the engineering of a sturdy structure or of necessary heating and cooling; architecture must do those things, but along a path of artistry.

Unlike many creative endeavors such as writing a novel, conceiving a recipe, designing fashion, or painting a masterpiece, architecture has a principled and idealistic agenda while also being responsible to budget, schedule, and codes of life safety—as well as being a servant to gravity, natural resources, and Mother Nature.

Goethe famously said, "Architecture is frozen music," and Jacob Voorthuis more currently suggested, "Music is melting architecture."

Either way, architecture is not a painting because it is three-dimensional. Architecture is not sculpture, because it is more than an object you engage by walking around. Akin to permanent installation and experiential art, architecture is a space and a place that one moves through in time, maybe once, maybe over and over again.

Architecture is a journey and a work of art that exists to attract and serve. Architecture has beauty, has form, and has function.

In its making, architecture can be created slowly and methodically in the same manner as a surgeon labors through a painstakingly complex procedure. Architecture can be created strategically and through experience, in the same manner as a general prepares for a battle. Or architecture can be created spontaneously, similar to the jazz musician who plays a tune without a preconceived ending.

The design idea that gives architecture its essence can come from history and the intensive study of precedents. The design idea can develop from days and weeks or maybe months of drawing in a sketchbook. It can begin with a single person's flash of brilliance or from the creative chemistry of a team of diverse talents. Ideas can appear overnight or take forever to form. The design and realization of a project can take a month, or it can take years, or even decades. For projects of universal greatness, full understanding requires generations.

Architecture is persistence, courage, optimism, and passion, along with a bit of insanity.

What other field sits at the intersection of art, science, business, and even human survival? What other field provides emotional, spiritual, and intellectual responses as well as a roof over our heads?

Aside from a need for protection, security, and shelter, why has humankind always had the passion to build and build—and build? In so many cities, why continue building taller and taller? When New York's Empire State Building was completed in 1929, we had the most beautiful and advanced skyscraper. At 1,250 feet tall, it was a work of art and accomplishment. Civilization proved itself confident and bold. In 2010 in Dubai, United Arab Emirates, a taller building was completed. At 2,700 feet in height, the Burj Khalifa is more than twice the height of the Empire State Building.

As I said, perhaps insanity.

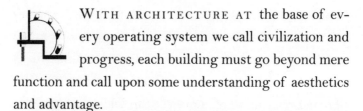 WITH ARCHITECTURE AT the base of every operating system we call civilization and progress, each building must go beyond mere function and call upon some understanding of aesthetics and advantage.

Imagine your existence without the structures that are integral to your daily life.

We need places to live, and we want these places to be heartfelt and hospitable. We need places to go to work, and we want these places to be comfortable and efficient. We need schools, and we want these places to be encouraging and supportive. Our neighborhoods need places to gather, and we want these places to be democratic and energized. Our communities need churches to worship in, and we want these places to be inspirational and transcendent. Our businesses need places to thrive, and we want these places to be strategic and informed. Our politicians need places to debate, and we want these places to ignite strength and influence. As a critical discipline, architecture is something we all need.

WHEN I WAS a child, as I suspect is true for many architects, it started with Lego bricks and some pen and paper. As a five-year-old, I created things. I built worlds of incredible fantasy and detail. I drew cities and civilizations that had purpose. As I grew older, my visions were captured with clay, cardboard, any form of physical material on which I could get my hands. I continued to dream and sculpt worlds of peace and progress. I envisioned places for people to live, to grow, to fall in love, and to find meaning in their life.

Then one day, like a flash of vivid lightning striking my brain, my heart, and my hands, I realized that there was a pursuit in life that could make many of my dreams, visions, and artistic explorations into reality. Architecture.

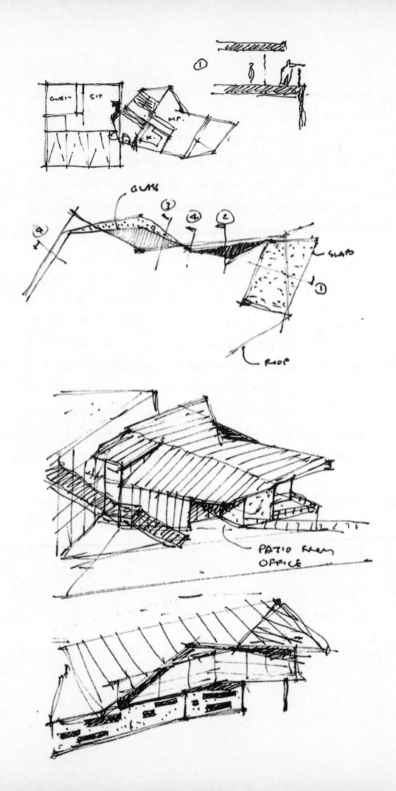

FIVE CITIES LOOKING

I have never felt salvation in nature.
I love cities above all.

MICHELANGELO

Prologue

I move and I dance, because I cannot stay still. I constantly seek the things that I forgot, the things that patiently wait to be found. My heart beating a bit faster, a bit louder, I know that I will soon have these things. Once possessed, all things stay with me; I trust they will—here, somewhere, anywhere I might go.

SAN FRANCISCO, CALIFORNIA

A tour book once told me this: It is a shame when native San Franciscans grow up and leave the city, because they then realize that the rest of the world is not as beautiful or as perfect as the San Francisco from which they came.

San Francisco may be a paradise found. Maybe.

AS A CHILD, I rolled oranges down the legendary hills of this sculpted city. I chose my oranges from a massive field of other oranges, to be freed. Immediately upon arriving home from the fruit stand, I released these spherical bodies. To go downhill, hill after hill, reaching inevitably the watery beginnings of the San Francisco Bay, was the oranges' given course.

Perhaps I lived each day as the oranges did, and perhaps San Francisco had chosen me—like I chose the oranges—to be freed.

 I LOST MYSELF to the city. I placed myself inside confusion, an inviting disorientation that challenges equilibrium and naive complacency. To lose myself in concentrated neighborhoods was like looking for an end in some kind of urban infinity. North or south, east or west, up or down, left or right—I did not know which way was which, which way was out.

I became relatively *small*, enjoying the chance to be discreet and inconspicuous. In San Francisco, I chose to retreat. I chose the comfort it provided. I chose to hide by letting the city take me.

I walked down an alley—deep, dark, and uninviting. In it were pockets of surprise: storefronts, people, games, activities, and so on—convincing me that an entire community was hiding in this unsuspecting crack of earth.

Years passed, and I traced my way back to this alley. It had been made sort of pretty. A municipal service had repaved the way with ivory concrete, cleaned and painted its cramped walls, and installed streetlamps for those who were afraid of the dark.

This alley, now supposedly rejuvenated, lost all its charms, all its surprises, all its desirable contradictions. The previous danger hiding its treasure was now covered under layers of modern civilization—a street community suffocating under "best intentions."

I realized later that in this small surround, the number of alleys outnumbered the main and known streets by manyfold. So many alleys to find. So many experiences to confront.

So many oranges.

 THERE IS SOMETHING to be said about San Francisco's relentless cloak of fog. Having been delivered "on little cat feet," as Carl Sandburg wrote, is an inevitable part of any dreamscape. By cloaking reality, it creates mystery, as if someone forced a large crevice into the psyche. It polarizes what one sees and what one should see, what one knows and what one should know. This discrepancy then must make one wonder if urban existence is meant to be explicit or implicit.

MOST WORKDAYS AT the lunch hour, I left the office and drove to the docks, the apparent end of the city. Having found a lonely dock, I parked my car and stared into vast waters. I still feel small when I face the majesty of the San Francisco Bay. Invariably I have the vertiginous sensation of wanting to drive my car just a few feet forward and be one with majesty—but then lunch would be an eternal break.

In those days, I felt there was something odd about the city hills at my back, as if the weight of this mountainous urbanscape were pushing me forward to the seam between earth and water, between dock and bay, between everything I know and everything I do not.

The city holds me still at that which painfully divides a city-sized outcropping of rock we call San Francisco from the depths of the bay. One side of this edge pushes out, exposing its most intimate secrets in the face of modern civilization. The other side recedes, as if its body is sheer void.

I sit perched between two animated forces.

Again I have to wonder. If I look to retreat from the gripping toils of my daily scenario, why then have I placed myself within such toiling grips? I am not certain why I escape into conflict. Maybe I simply fabricate imaginary conflict so as to place it next to my own petty ones. This way, perhaps I test to see if my emotional poise will buckle.

AT THE MARINA, a finger of land stretches from behind buildings and elongates onto the water's surface. Surrounded by crashing waves, earth is sculpted into an intimate gathering spot called the "Wave Organ." Because the seating areas are made of earth itself—its meat and refuge both—to relax here was like trying to get away by staying put.

There was a tension between being nestled in a form of land and art while also being encompassed by dark, intent waters. A single burst of ocean waves could make me aware of my precarious position between the nothingness of the sky and that of the sea. There was nothing else, except my prosaic and insignificant worries. How petty and small I must be.

 THE GRANDNESS OF these great things—a city's intimate secrets hidden in Italianate hills, a dock poised on watery oblivion, a speck of land balanced between sky and sea—and an infinite wealth of others—made my own personal hardships contemptible.

What I have is What-I-Have, and what I have is mine alone either to worship or to deny, obsess over or negate. It would be fair, then, to have my sometimes trivial passions confront much greater forces; to know that I matter and to realize that all things great and small move through me, find balance inside my own desires.

BERKELEY, CALIFORNIA

I woke up every morning earlier than most. At the start of my day, I would sit at a piano in an anonymous practice room—an underground room nurtured by Earth's hug. Hidden in the basement of the music building, these practice rooms were said to be an acoustically insulated soundproof environment. Such is necessary for musical concentration.

But for all the padding and fabric tucked into the walls, for all the acoustic tiles dangling from the ceiling, for all the silicone sealing the door and peep window, these rooms were not at all soundproof.

Rather, the opposite.

Somehow, these rooms invited in all the noises harbored nearby to practice with me. I heard all the musical and unmusical sounds from next door. I heard all the talking in the halls. I heard all the slamming of locker doors.

Instead of having a private rehearsal session, I submitted to the apparent lack of intimacy. I played my piano with the violinist next door, the singer on the other side of the hall, and the percussionist across the way. I played with an "orchestra" of random and unintentional collaboration. I played with an assemblage of chance musicians unaware they were now included in a larger musical scheme of things.

First I would listen, then I would echo or mimic. Maybe taunt.

Then, with egomaniacal bravado, I would try to out-perform the other musicians who sat inches from me, separated by what was intended to be a severe partition. We sat apart and together, absurdly. Individually seated in our own practice rooms, we played collectively in some great hall of communal sound: directionless, leaderless, a field of ridiculous resonance.

SOMETIMES THE DAY did not go so well. I really needed to get away.

Named "Indian Rock," this place of escape served me well. In the midst of a cluster of small homes sat a powerful outcropping of boulders larger than the neighboring houses.

Here I climbed to the pinnacle, and here I sat on Mother Earth. As the mountainous rocks jutted through the delicate skin of this city, I tried to forget that my nervous day jutted through my very own delicate skin, piercing both mind and heart.

I sat on these rocks, the bare surface of the earth warm to my touch. Despite the rock's height, I was warmed by the furnace deep in the planet's core. High enough to look over the little houses below, I pondered the tiny shelters of domesticity, these fabricated wood bubbles.

I sat unsheltered under cold night of dark sky. I sat on Mother Earth's warming heart. Maybe together—the maternal warmth beneath me and the poignant chill above—could soothe my worries. I was gently placed between these two animated forces. As I was in San Francisco.

New York, New York

Flying. West Coast to East Coast. I flew from a small place to a much larger one, a larger place with a frenzied pace already set in motion, prearranged just for me. I deplaned like a child taking that eager first leap onto the moving steps of an escalator.

Not wasting time, one must sense the rhythm and jump with a certain amount of faith. If the child at the escalator guesses wrong, there is little opportunity to readjust. Falling, collapsing, his spirit crushed, body off balance, he will still be carried forward by the mechanical beast.

I WAS MINDFUL of a movie that impressed upon my imagination an idyllic New York City. The people in these flickering images went out to the city streets and were transformed, became the moisture on slick, reflective, dark passages. Like flurries of snow, they drifted where the wind blew them, lingered in places where other flakes had already stuck. Or, like the humidity of an August day, these people stilled the beating city to a sluggish silence.

I moved to New York to play, like the glossy film actors who make all movements and gestures—even to scratch the itch on the nose—exciting.

URBAN SNOW IS just short of magic. When my first snow came, I was struck by a strange feeling of weightlessness. The night streets were covered in a blanket of white. The streetlights beamed down. The city unleashed a gentle spirit.

In this dark night, it was peculiar that the snow reflected light upward. The snow-covered street with its reflected glow was itself a source of light.

Imagine walking on light. Imagine sources of light not just on the ground but on the buildings and rooftops as well. Everywhere. And most magically, because the area was so evenly lit, there were no shadows.

Every piece of this mighty city was ungrounded. Things were no longer part of a whole, no longer part of a universal truth that was defined by some myth called light-and-shadow. And gravity.

Things were simply left sitting gently, suspiciously, and purposelessly. No reason to be here or there. It seemed as if God could, by letting a slight breath of his nostrils blow, move parts of this town like mere particles of dust.

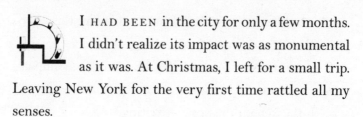 I HAD BEEN in the city for only a few months. I didn't realize its impact was as monumental as it was. At Christmas, I left for a small trip. Leaving New York for the very first time rattled all my senses.

I caught the subway to the airport. That was cheapest, to travel in passages dug out of dirt, water, and granite. Like rodents, we sneaked around beneath the impressive weight of New York City. For one dollar, I received a subway token and placed myself deep in urbanity, so intensely inside.

The monumental moment was brief.

When the subway train pulled out from the grave tunnels and I rode outside and above the ground, I saw light. Space. Landscape. Distance. Trees.

My God, I saw trees. My God, I saw distance.

I saw a suburbanscape stretching for miles. I did not see the usual skyline of Manhattan, the one in which I walk only a few steps and the next big building is in my view. In my way.

Now, out of Earth's shafts, the light was blinding, as if God wanted me to know that all heaven had broken loose. The infinite amount of space was overwhelming. My body shook with relief and shock, as if someone had released my disturbed, convicted soul.

I had been inside the city too long—inside some perverse kind of concrete-and-steel bulk, underground in a metal container, walking endless streets and passages that made little sense, hoping that sun and rain might slip between buildings to reach my face. Whether I was in the city or beneath it, to have any part of this island is a cavernous circumstance. I realize that now.

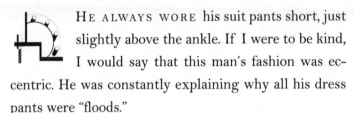 HE ALWAYS WORE his suit pants short, just slightly above the ankle. If I were to be kind, I would say that this man's fashion was eccentric. He was constantly explaining why all his dress pants were "floods."

"It's simple," he said, gesturing like a crazy man. "I wear floods because New York City is a sinking ship. I need to prepare myself for the incoming rush of ocean waves."

Every so often, people claim that New York City is not what it used to be. San Francisco, as well, is not what it used to be. Or simply, no great metropolitan city is what it used to be.

Some say cities around the world are deteriorating, falling from pedestals of world culture into shelters for social waste. From tales of day-to-day urban inspiration to sin and dismay, these once great cities collapse.

I have to argue differently; I have to offer a different posture.

Sure. The great American cities are "sinking"; so too are the European ones, as well as cities in every country.

Cambridge, Massachusetts

If I remember correctly, it went something like this. Out in the town square sat "the Chess Master." To play him in a game of chess, you would first pay him two dollars. If you lost, he kept your money, and if you were lucky or skillful enough to win, the master gave you back your two dollars.

Paying money for him to win, you paid for knowledge—two dollars' worth.

I was often bored in Cambridge, and because boredom is like some kind of spiritual death, it forces me frantically to do things. Any things.

Los Angeles, California

I am not sure how often I have made the drive from San Francisco to Los Angeles, from Los Angeles to San Francisco. It seems like thousands at least. The drive is endless and ever unchanging, monotony at its best. Slightly more than four hundred miles, the trip is short enough to make one believe it might be comfortable but long enough to test one's tolerance for continual emptiness.

Nothing on Highway 5 marks progress. It is empty. Straight, flat, barren, vacuous, barely inhabited. As I drive hour upon hour, this journey hollows itself out with each passing mile. The hum of the automobile cruising at 80 mph becomes a deity, because here, one worships any evidence of reality.

In the briskly moving car, the clocks and watches tick on. Outside, nothing has importance. Outside this mechanical animal of glass, metal, and rubber, the world seems to have come to a mysterious abrupt halt. From this raging vehicle, looking for signs of life is like violently motioning for salvation in a dark space, hoping that someone or something will come and put the passing of life and time back in order.

I am sealed tightly in a glass jar, and someone has hurled me into a frictionless space. With only an end and only a beginning, I travel inside perpetual nothingness. I am bracketed in a sharp gap between two cities. If my forever floating jar finally hits its target, it will shatter.

ON ONE TRIP, arriving in Los Angeles, I noticed immediately that time had stopped. Not that life stopped, but the passing of time had truly ceased. One day was simply the same as the next.

This curious unyielding state with no beginning, middle, or end was what Sisyphus might call existence, or what Beethoven might call his last string quartets.

All this made life empty yet forgivingly eternal. Life became easy. Who would not want life that is easy? Who would not want life that is pleasant? Life should not always challenge the soul, breaking it down until it cries out. I now have something called character.

I forget the movie, but I do faintly remember one particular scene. Each morning is so charmed that the actress knows only to step out into the sun glow and say, "Another fucking beautiful day."

Every LA morning now I awake and walk out onto my sun-drenched balcony, into the God-given rays of warmth and light.

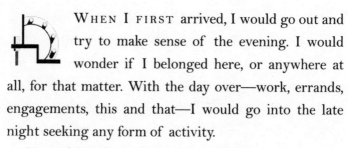WHEN I FIRST arrived, I would go out and try to make sense of the evening. I would wonder if I belonged here, or anywhere at all, for that matter. With the day over—work, errands, engagements, this and that—I would go into the late night seeking any form of activity.

Everything that existed after midnight was not very real to me, though I was very real to them. A blur of uneventful events, there were people everywhere, doing everything, hoping to find rhyme and reason.

Four thirty a.m. Very soon the faint beams of the sun will edge over the horizon. This will announce everyone's death-like fatigue. I do not know where I am or who I am. Or if I will ever belong.

NOISE AND SILENCE go hand in hand. When I think of noisy days, I do not just think of taxis, or subways, or a screaming circus of people. I think of noise as a personal relationship, or maybe the hectic pace of things-to-do.

Contrarily, when I think of silent days, I do not just think of riding in my insulated automobile. I also think of the aggressive waves of the Pacific Ocean crashing into the edges of Los Angeles.

Pablo Casals often spoke of music this way: that it is not just the notes that make music but the silence between them as well.

As there is a yearning gap of noiselessness in music—this gap that gropes to be filled—there is in urbanity a constant field of noise, waiting to be filled with silence and peace. Both noise and silence need space, and each comfortably fits around the other.

As the tale goes, the unwitnessed falling tree makes no sound. I would argue that it makes no silence either.

Epilogue

I have always carried with me two things: naive confidence and a mad desire to have something/anything happen to me. The latter is dangerously silly, this I know, but I am fearful of boredom and complacency. I want to have stories to tell. I have sought adventure, both real and imagined. I have sought attention, both encouraging and narcissistic.

"Love me or hate me, but don't ignore me."

Whether it is danger, confrontation, or simply the lyrical garbage in the streets, I have needed things to happen to me and scream into my mind's ear that I am alive and living a wholehearted existence.

When I die, I want to know that things happened to me, as well as that I happened to things. I need to know that my life was rich, involved, substantial, intentional, and, I would say most of all, authentic.

I guess I should accuse myself of melancholy, or even more, of being overly sentimental. I would rather be rightfully accused of such things than suspected of being empty.

If my mind constantly moves and there is nowhere to go, then so be it. Let it move in sentimental circles, for I am not afraid of fetishizing my own sentiments. I am not afraid of gutting my heart so as to know for certain that I indeed have one. I am not afraid of exposing my thoughts. This way I know for certain that I, once in a while, possess thoughts.

 As I LOOK for the same things in different cities, as I look at the cities I have faced with a passion, I see that the cities look back at me. They would like to know what I am looking for. I can only say that I desire a chance to look at my very own movement through life.

I like passing through cities and having cities pass through me. It is about the same events occurring in different contexts. Contrasting times and places make repeated acts worthwhile, like the second or third reading of good literature.

The need to hide from certain monsters brought me to these few different places. Whether it was to run and hide, or to seek and follow, or to lead and discover, I arrived.

The monsters that trample my heart, the skeletons that rattle in my closet, and the creatures that creep through my luggage do not control me, but they force me to keep moving. I pay attention to these monsters because nobody has yet shown me a better, or more honest, way to cope.

My monsters are at least that: honest. Though I sometimes run, I know they chase me, or more often guide me, to where I should go anyway.

Whether because of these places I have mentioned here or other places I have visited, I like to tell myself that I have always been resourceful. I convince myself that my personal resources, stamina, and eager heart have sought out all that was to be found, all that would fill this mind and body, and all that would tease my hungry imagination.

To move once again, I can wait no longer.

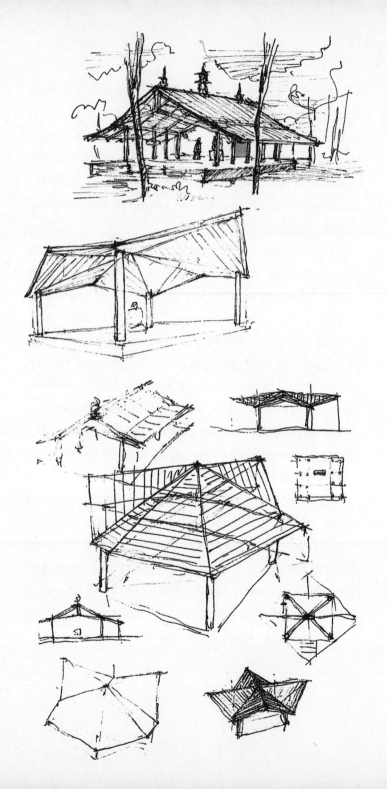

THE TEMPLE

Humility is not thinking less of yourself.
It's thinking of yourself less.

RICK WARREN

WHETHER CREATED FOR a family in a house, students at a school, or employees of a company, architecture does much more than simply cover, enclose, and protect. It nurtures us, helps us to be better people.

In the arc of extremes, stone and beams make the fortress more immune to attack; steel and glass make an office tower rise over the rest; and wood and shingle make a sturdy but warm home. In the middle of the spectrum, stone and steel and wood can combine to house centuries of learning or keep the homeless safe one more night.

For whoever comes together to use a structure, the architecture serves as a vessel of experiences and events. Architecture creates a place to rest. To learn. To think. To grow. To connect.

That is what the term "architecture" means to me, what I strive for every day in my life's work. The materials are just the means to an end. It is whom the structure is for and how it all comes together in my head, then on paper, then on the ground and up into the air, finally, to be used by people in their own lives' endeavors that makes architecture a noble, useful, and vital enterprise.

THE POWER OF architecture to heal and improve lives became fully realized for me in 2008 when I was asked to design several buildings for a forty-five-acre Buddhist retreat in the stunning Shenandoah Mountains of Virginia.

Though I respect and even envy those who have found meanings and answers that I have not, though I am spiritual and religious, I am not a Buddhist. Still, a high school friend who was a member of a Buddhist group and knew the range of my work asked if I'd be interested in coming east to see the land and the setting, meet the leader of the group, and discuss their ideas for a small temple and other structures.

As an architect, of course I have a vision of how a project might look, sail, exceed expectations. But architecture is about listening.

Listening intently.

The public's perception of architecture—and of

most architects—is of vain master builders working on a grand scale. Their public projects of outrageously bent steel, overwhelming glass facades, and irresponsible budgets make the newspapers and magazines. But grandiose projects such as those strike me as being based on ego and fame, not listening. And as a result, they take form by imposing an outsider's own vision of a project in a way that often does not fit its surroundings. Sure, I have been found guilty of this selfishness, but not here.

 MY EXPERIENCE IN the mountains of Virginia with the Buddhists was of creative joy and collaboration, of a higher purpose, and, most important, of listening. It was a rare opportunity to work in a peaceful setting with people who exude calm and clarity. My initial charge: to design three buildings to serve the organization's mission of providing guidance in meditation and philosophy.

I was a lucky man.

The late Shamar Rinpoche, the fourteenth Shamarpa and Red Hat Lama of Tibet, personally guided me on the projects. As a teacher and founder of Bodhi Path schools around the United States and the world, he had set as the mission of his work—and of this retreat in the mountains—to explore the teachings of the Buddha so as to understand better the mind and human emotions.

The purpose of the retreat was "bringing kindness and discernment to everyday situations."

It isn't every day one works personally with a high Tibetan lama descended from a line of holy men going back to the thirteenth century. Our meetings were intimate, though diverse in venue: at the Los Angeles offices of Poon Design with others of my studio team; in Virginia, surrounded by Rinpoche's associates; over dinner at my home in the Hollywood Hills with my children; or by phone when he was in Asia, traveling to speak to his thousands of followers.

We often sketched building designs together. Completely at ease with a drawing pen in hand, Rinpoche produced simple but insightful sketches to express his visions for a new Buddhist retreat.

 HOW THESE PROJECTS evolved over the years reflects much of what I feel is the goodness and humility of architecture and design.

We completed the meditation retreat house, then the temple, then a small support building near the temple, after which I started work on the dining hall, a multipurpose building with a large assembly space that will capture panoramic views of mountains and trees. Downstairs will be retail, offices, and guest quarters. Large grassy fields for community gatherings will surround the building.

Rinpoche passed away in the middle of this project. I was fortunate to have had many one-on-one exchanges with him. Thousands of people wait their whole lives to be in his presence. I am forever grateful for Rinpoche, in my house, playing with my daughters, and his influence forever in our hearts.

ACKNOWLEDGMENTS

Thank you to my oldest and dearest friend, Christine Fang, who has believed in me since we were kids. To Carl Lennertz, my mentor and editor, who believed in this manuscript and brought it to life. To Betsy Lane and Marge Eberts, whose initial notes had me imagine that I actually might have a real book. To my publisher, Fred Ramey of Unbridled Books, who has been a brilliant and generous guiding force in the shaping of the final book. And to my agent, Sandra Bond of Bond Literary Agency, for steering me through the literary industry.

I acknowledge my friends Vince Jordan, Danny Yee and Mina Chow, who upon hearing the ideas for this book found interest and gave support. They showed me that this book might have an audience. David E. Martin, mentor, colleague, and friend, revealed to me that grace and giving surpassed good design. Thank you for that. Greg Lombardi, dear friend, artistic collaborator, and partner in life, you have been missed.

My heartfelt gratitude is given to the team of Poon Design, where every day we embark on adventures together. Led by Principal John Kim, our team includes Sandy Lee, Esther Chung, Shani Cho, Bryan Bethem, Jared Licano, Ben Kalenik, Noreena Manio, Seth Trotter, Barbara Leon, Carlos Hernandez, Jim Gilette, Debra Hakimi, Niloo Hosseini, Anushri Vachhani, Charles Proffitt, and many more. My studio is also considered family with my closest collaborators: Robert Weimer, Elizabeth Low, Danny and Sue Yee, and Cynthia Kraus.

To the Denver Publishing Institute for inviting me to meet the class and to have my first "signing" (of the early manuscript), and to four graduates who were early readers and commenters on the book: Amie Flanagan, Jennifer Schafer, Mary Westover, and Ashley Waterman.

To all those mentioned in my book—from friends, colleagues, teachers, and mentors to employers and employees, clients, agencies, and cities—I thank you all for providing me the substance that comprises my life as an architect. You have given me gifts of humor, inspiration, and some battle scars.

Finally and of course, I thank my wife, Martha Eberts, and my two brilliant and silly daughters, Ella and Lily, who inspire me to do boundless things.

ANTHONY POON

LIST OF COMPLETED PROJECTS

www.poondesign.com

As of November 11, 2015

CULTURAL/RELIGIOUS

Buddhist Temple, Wisdom Foundation, Blue Ridge Mountains, Virginia, 2013

Beverly Hills Visitor Center, Beverly Hills, California, 2012

Meditation Retreat House, Wisdom Foundation, Blue Ridge Mountains, Virginia, 2010

Denver Museum of Nature and Science new atrium lobby, exhibit halls, and planetarium, Denver, Colorado, 2003 (with HHPA)

EDUCATIONAL: HIGHER EDUCATION

Library, the American University in Cairo, Egypt, 2009 (with HHPA)

Institute for Collaboration, Aurora University, Aurora, Illinois, 2008 (with A4E)[1]

Harrington Learning Commons, Sobrato Technology Center and Orradre Library, Santa Clara University, California, 2008 (with HHPA)

Northwest Campus Student Housing, University of California, Los Angeles, 2007 (with HHPA)

Wooden West, University of California, Los Angeles, 2005 (with HHPA)

DeBartolo Performing Arts Center, University of Notre Dame, Indiana, 2003 (with HHPA)

Student Activities Center, University of California, Los Angeles, 2003 (with HHPA)

Pima County Community Colleges, Tucson, Arizona, 2002 (with HHPA)

Richter Library renovation and addition, University of Miami, Florida, 2002 (with HHPA)

Recreation Center, Soka University of America, Aliso Viejo, California, 2001 (with HHPA)

Residence Halls, Soka University of America, Aliso Viejo, California, 2001 (with HHPA)

University Hall, California State University, Northridge, 2000 (with HHPA)

Cintas Center, Xavier University, Cincinnati, Ohio, 1999 (with NBBJ)

EDUCATIONAL: K–12

Esteban Torres High School, Los Angeles, California, 2010 (with A4E)

High school renovation and additions, San Lorenzo Unified School District, California, 2009 (with A4E)

Valley Academy of the Arts and Sciences, Granada Hills, California, 2008 (with A4E)

Feather River Academy, Sutter County School District, Yuba City, California, 2006 (with A4E)[2]

View Park High School, Los Angeles, California, 2004 (with A4E)

SCHOOL DISTRICT 129

Herget Middle School, School District 129, Aurora, Illinois, 2005 (with A4E)[3]

Freeman Elementary School, School District 129, Aurora, Illinois, 2004 (with A4E)

Goodwin Elementary School, School District 129, Aurora, Illinois, 2004 (with A4E)

Greenman Elementary School, School District 129, Aurora, Illinois, 2004 (with A4E)[4]

Hall Elementary School, School District 129, Aurora, Illinois, 2004 (with A4E)

Hill Elementary School, School District 129, Aurora, Illinois, 2004 (with A4E)

Jefferson Middle School, School District 129, Aurora, Illinois, 2004 (with A4E)

Lincoln Elementary School, School District 129, Aurora, Illinois, 2004 (with A4E)

McCleery Elementary School, School District 129, Aurora, Illinois, 2004 (with A4E)

Nicholson Elementary School, School District 129, Aurora, Illinois, 2004 (with A4E)

Schneider Elementary School, School District 129, Aurora, Illinois, 2004 (with A4E)

Smith Elementary School, School District 129, Aurora, Illinois, 2004 (with A4E)

Washington Middle School, School District 129, Aurora, Illinois, 2004 (with A4E)

West High School, School District 129, Aurora, Illinois, 2004

COMMERCIAL/HOSPITALITY

Combined Properties renovation, Beverly Hills, California, 2015

Enzoani, Riyadh, Saudi Arabia, 2015

Heritage Fine Wines, Beverly Hills, California, 2015

Alta Verde Group, Century City, California, 2014

Din Tai Fung, South Coast Plaza, Costa Mesa, California, 2014

Fleurish Flower Bar, Los Angeles, California, 2014

Vosges Chocolate Factory, Chicago, Illinois, 2014[5]

Aura Cycle, Los Angeles, California, 2013

Din Tai Fung, The Americana at Brand, Glendale, California, 2013

Indus, Los Angeles, California, 2013

Mendocino Farms, Fig at 7th, Los Angeles, California, 2013

Mendocino Farms, 3rd and Fairfax, Los Angeles, California, 2013

Sugarfina, Beverly Hills, California, 2013

Beverly Hills Visitor Center, Beverly Hills, California, 2012

Blue Cow, Los Angeles, California, 2012

Klueger & Stein, LLP, Encino, California, 2012

Mendocino Farms, West Hollywood, California, 2012

Saffron, Baldwin Hills, California, 2012

Saffron, Los Angeles, California, 2011

Santa Monica + La Brea renovation, West Hollywood, California, 2011

SMPY renovation, Santa Monica, California, 2011

Stone Oven, Los Angeles, California, 2011

Sunny Blue, Santa Monica, California, 2011

Sushi Noguchi, Yorba Linda, California, 2011[6]

Vosges Haut-Chocolat, Beverly Hills, California, 2011

Deluca's Italian Deli, The Americana at Brand, Glendale, California, 2010

Mendocino Farms MDR, Marina Del Rey, California, 2010[7]

Saffron, Beverly Hills, California, 2010

8 Fish, Los Angeles, California, 2009

Chaya Downtown, Los Angeles, California, 2009[8]

Drago Centro exterior canopy, Los Angeles, California, 2009

Larson, Garrick & Lightfoot, Law Offices, Los Angeles, California, 2009

Memphis Café, Manhattan Beach, California, 2009

Mendocino Farms 444, 444 South Flower, Los Angeles, California, 2009

W-V Mixed-Use Project, Manhattan Beach, California, 2009

Joss Cuisine, Beverly Hills, California, 2008

SMPY warehouse, Santa Monica, California, 2008

Santa Monica Power Yoga, Santa Monica, California, 2007

Geary's, Beverly Hills, California, 1998 (with KAA)[9]

Nicole Miller, Boca Raton, Florida, 1998 (with KAA)

Avant Garde, Beverly Hills, California, 1996 (with KAA)

TwoPart café, Los Angeles, California, 1992

URBAN/PUBLIC/MASTER PLANNING

Northwest Campus Student Housing, University of California, Los Angeles, 2007 (with HHPA)

School District 129, Aurora, Illinois, 2004 (with A4E)
Anaheim Cultural District, Anaheim, California, 2002 (with HHPA)
Pima County Community Colleges, Tucson, Arizona, 2002 (with HHPA)
Good Shepherd Center for Homeless Women & Children, Los Angeles,
  California, 1996 (with KAA)[10]
Hermosa Beach Pier, California, 1994[11]

SPORTS/ENTERTAINMENT

Recreation Center, Soka University of America, Aliso Viejo, California,
  2002 (with HHPA)
Cintas Center, Xavier University, Cincinnati, Ohio, 1999 (with NBBJ)

FURNITURE DESIGN

Din Tai Fung, South Coast Plaza, Costa Mesa, California, 2014
Din Tai Fung, The Americana at Brand, Glendale, California, 2013
W / Z Residence, Santa Monica, California, 2012
Sushi Noguchi, Yorba Linda, California, 2011[12]
Mendocino Farms MDR, Marina Del Rey, California, 2010[13]
Deluca's Italian Deli, The Americana at Brand, Glendale, California,
  2010
Mendocino Farms MDR, Marina Del Rey, California, 2010
S / B Residence, Encino, California, 2010
Chaya Downtown, Los Angeles, California, 2009[14]
Larson, Garrick & Lightfoot, Law Offices, Los Angeles, California, 2009
Mendocino Farms 444, Los Angeles, California, 2009
Santa Monica Power Yoga, Santa Monica, California, 2007
TwoPart café, Los Angeles, California, 1992

RESIDENTIAL

Escena West residential development, Palm Springs, California, 2015
Villa Sunset, Los Angeles, California, 2015
Monte Sereno residential development, Palm Springs, California, 2014[15]

Alta Verde Escena residential development, Palm Springs, California, 2013[16]

Coral Mountain residential development, La Quinta, California, 2013[17]

L / Y Residence, South Pasadena, California, 2012

Bliss Residence, Bel Air, California, 2011

K Residence, Porter Ranch, California, 2010

Meditation Retreat House, Wisdom Foundation, Blue Ridge Mountains, Virginia, 2010

S / B Residence, Encino, California, 2010

W / Z Residence, Santa Monica, California, 2010

WV Mixed-Use Project, Manhattan Beach, California, 2009

B Residence, Hope Ranch, California, 2008

RNB Renovation, Los Angeles, California, 2008

Northwest Campus Student Housing, University of California, Los Angeles, 2007 (with HHPA)

Hollywood Hills Residence, Los Angeles, California 2002

Residence Halls, Soka University of America, Aliso Viejo, California, 2001 (with HHPA)

Endnotes

1. Outstanding Design Award, American School & University magazine, 2008.

2. Citation Award, The American Institute of Architects Committee on Architecture for Education Educational Facility Design, California, 2007.

3. Grand Prize, NSBA National Exhibition of School Architecture, 2007; Citation of Excellence, Learning by Design, 2007; Award of Distinction for "Excellence in the Design of Educational Environments," Association of School Boards, 2007; 2006 Exhibition of Educational Environments at the Joint Annual Conference of IASB, IASA, and IASBO, 2007; Honorable Mention, Education Design Showcase, School Planning & Management, 2007; Award, Impact on Learning, 2007; Merit Award, DesignShare, School Construction News, Edutopia, and Schools for Life, 2006.

4. Grand Prize, NSBA National Exhibition of School Architecture, 2006; Honorable Mention, Outstanding Architecture and Design in Education, School Planning & Management, 2006; 2006 Exhibition of Educational Environments, Joint Annual Conference of

IASB, IASA, and IASBO, 2006; Merit Award, American Institute of Architects, Inland California Chapter, California, 2005; 2005 Honor Society, KnowledgeWorks Foundation, 2005; Merit Award, DesignShare and School Construction News, 2005; Impact on Learning Award, School & College Planning & Management, 2005; Grand Prize, Learning by Design National Highest Honor, 2005; Design Citation, Architectural Portfolio, American School & University magazine, 2004.

5. Award Winner, Industrial Redevelopment of the Year; Awards of Excellence, National Association of Industrial and Office Parks Chicago, Illinois, 2013.

6. Finalist for Design Award for Best Restaurant, The American Institute of Architects, Los Angeles Chapter, California, 2012.

7. International Design Award for Best Restaurant, People's Choice, The American Institute of Architects, Los Angeles Chapter, California, 2011.

8. International Design Award for Best Restaurant, The American Institute of Architects, Los Angeles Chapter, California, 2009.

9. Architectural Award, The Los Angeles Business Council, Twenty-Eighth Annual Urban Beautification Architectural Awards Program, California, 1998.

10. Merit Award, The American Institute of Architects, South Bay Chapter, California, 1997.

11. Merit Award, The American Institute of Architects, Cabrillo Chapter, California, 1995.

12. Finalist for Design Award for Best Restaurant, The American Institute of Architects, Los Angeles Chapter, California, 2012.

13. International Design Award for Best Restaurant, People's Choice, The American Institute of Architects, Los Angeles Chapter, California, 2011.

14. International Design Award for Best Restaurant, The American Institute of Architects, Los Angeles Chapter, California, 2009.

15. Design Lens Excellence Award, National Peer Group, John Burns Real Estate Consulting, 2005; Award of Merit, Best Single Family Detached Home, Gold Nugget Awards, Pacific Coast Builders Conference, 2014; National Gold Award, Best Detached Home, Best of 50+, National Association of Home Builders, 2014.

16. National Silver Award, Best Single Family Home, National Association of Home Builders, 2014; National Gold Award, Detached Home Built for-Sale, Best in American Living, National Association of Home Builders, 2013; Finalist, Best Architecture Design, Single Family Home, Icon Awards, Building Industry Association, 2013; Award of Merit, Best Single Family Detached Home, Gold Nugget Awards, Pacific Coast Builders Conference, 2013; Finalist for Reimagine Mid-Century Design, Dwell, 2013.

17. Award of Merit, Best Single Family Detached Home, Gold Nugget Awards, Pacific Coast Builders Conference, 2014; National Innovation Award, Best for-Sale Community, Best of 50+, National Association of Home Builders, 2014; National Silver Award, Best Detached Community, National Association of Home Builders, 2014; National Platinum Award, Detached Home Built for-Sale, Best in American Living, National Association of Home Builders, 2013; Best in Region, Pacific, Best in American Living, National Association of Home Builders, 2013.